Out of Order

A Comedy

Ray Cooney

A SAMUEL FRENCH ACTING EDITION

SAMUEL
FRENCH

FOUNDED 1830

SAMUELFRENCH-LONDON.CO.UK
SAMUELFRENCH.COM

ISBN 978-0-573-01858-9

www.samuelfrench-london.co.uk

www.samuelfrench.com

FOR AMATEUR PRODUCTION ENQUIRIES

UNITED KINGDOM AND WORLD
EXCLUDING NORTH AMERICA

plays@SamuelFrench-London.co.uk

020 7255 4302/01

Each title is subject to availability from Samuel French,

depending upon country of performance.

OUT OF ORDER

First produced (under the title *Whose Wife Is It Anyway?*) at the Thorndike Theatre, Leatherhead, on 8th May, 1990, with the following cast:

The Manager	John Pennington
Richard Willey MP	Bruce Montague
The Waiter	Robert Fyfe
The Maid	Sally Kinghorn
Jane Worthington	Judy Buxton
A Body	David Warwick
George Pigden	Ray Cooney
Ronnie Worthington	Michael Fenner
Pamela Willey	Wanda Ventham

Directed by Ray Cooney
Designed by Douglas Heap

Subsequently produced by The Theatre of Comedy Company at the Shaftesbury Theatre, London, on 28th September, 1990, with the following cast:

Richard Willey	Donald Sinden
The Manager	Dennis Ramsden
The Waiter	Brian Murphy
Jane Worthington	Sandra Dickinson
A Body	David Warwick
George Pigden	Michael Williams
The Maid	Pamela Cundell
Ronnie Worthington	Michael Fenner
Pamela Willey	Wanda Ventham
Gladys	Jaqueline Clarke

Directed by Ray Cooney
Designed by Douglas Heap
Lighting by James Baird

The action of the play takes place in suite 648 of the *Westminster Hotel*, London, about 8.30 pm on a September evening

Time—the present

CHARACTERS

Richard Willey, A sauve and successful man and a Junior Minister in the Government of the day
The Manager, A severe man
The Waiter, A nimble and wily old servant
The Maid, A plump Italian woman in her fifties
Jane Worthington, An attractive but dizzy young lady
A Body, A nondescript middle-aged man
George Pigden, An upright pleasant man of nervous disposition
Ronnie, An angry young man
Pamela, An attractive sophisticated woman in her forties
Gladys, A bossy but attractive woman in her forties

AUTHOR'S NOTES

It is important that the characters of "A Body", "Ronnie", "Pamela" and "Gladys" are listed as such in all programmes or cast lists.

At the time the play was written the Government was "Conservative" and "Labour" was in opposition. Should that situation be different at the time of production then the Producer/Director may alter the pertinent references. In this printed version I have 'depersonalised' the references to "The Prime Minister" and "The Leader of the Opposition". Anyone producing the play may feel it's better to refer to the incumbents by name.

All the window "bangs" in the production must be very loud. The best method is a separate "slap-stick" coinciding with the window falling. This applies even when one of the characters gets struck!

Photograph by Nick Weeks

ACT I

The lounge of suite 648 on the sixth floor of the "Westminster Hotel", London

The style is slightly faded Regency. The lounge is dominated by a single large casement window which runs at an angle from URC *to* DRC, *taking up half of the wall*

DR, *below the window is a door to the bedroom.* UC *is a door leading to a cupboard. In the centre of the wall* DL *is the main door of the suite leading into a corridor. On the opposite side of the corridor is seen the door to suite 650*

Outside the window is a balcony, about three feet deep, beyond which can be seen the skyline over the Thames from Westminster. The balcony runs off UL *and* UR

The furniture is in keeping with the style of the room. There is a low divan at DLC *and a small low armchair* DRC. *Below the main door is a built-in cupboard in which is the radio and TV. In addition, depending on space, there are tables, ornaments and pictures. At the left end of the divan is a table on which is the telephone. The table has a lower shelf on which can be seen the London telephone directories*

When the CURTAIN *rises the lights are on and the curtains are closed. Richard Willey is standing behind the telephone dialling a number. He finishes dialling and looks impatiently at his watch. His briefcase is on the divan*

Richard (*on the phone*) Hello, darling. . . . Yes, I've just this second checked in. Same old suite, six-four-eight. Everything all right at home? . . . Good. . . . I wish you were too, darling, but it's an all-night sitting so you wouldn't see much of me. . . . Well, you know how the Prime Minister relies on me. Look, I'd better ring off my sweet, it's half-past eight and the debate was just about to get under way. . . . I will. And you have a nice early night with Dick Francis. I must rush, darling. See you tomorrow afternoon.

There is a knock on the hall door

(*On the phone*) Hang on, there's somebody at the door. (*Calling*) Who is it?

Manager (*off*) It's the Manager.

Richard opens the door while continuing to talk

Richard Coming! (*On the phone*) I'd better go, my sweet, or the debate will have started.

The Manager enters

Manager Good-evening, Mr Willey.

Richard holds up his hand

Sorry, Mr Willey.

Richard (*on the phone*) What's that? ... It was the Manager ... (*To the Manager*) Mrs Willey sends her best wishes.

Manager How kind. Will you reciprocate?

Richard (*on the phone*) The Manager reciprocates ... (*To the Manager*) Mrs Willey says "how kind".

Manager How kind.

Richard (*on the phone*) I must go, darling. You curl up in bed with Mr Francis.

The Manager raises an eyebrow

... Bye, darling. Sweet dreams.

Richard puts the phone down and grabs his briefcase. During the ensuing dialogue he takes out papers and hastily checks them

Manager I trust everything is to your satisfaction, Mr Willey.

Richard Fine, fine.

Manager We've just had this suite re-decorated.

Richard The twenty years was up, was it?

Manager (*wagging a reproving finger*) Mr Willey!

Richard As long as you don't improve the plumbing.

Manager The plumbing?

Richard The central heating starting up in the morning is far more reliable than your alarm calls.

The Waiter enters carrying Richard's case

Ah, thank you. (*He tips the Waiter a coin*)

The Waiter looks at the coin, drops the case and exits

He's just about due for re-decorating, isn't he?

Manager Would you like an early morning call, Mr Willey?

Richard Not too early after an all-nighter. Nine o'clock will be fine.

Manager I'll arrange for the central heating to be turned on at nine precisely.

Richard is stuffing the papers into his briefcase

Richard I think I've got everything for the debate.

Manager Will you be making one of your blistering ministerial speeches?

Richard Only if the Opposition cuts up rough. (*Indicating the door*) You carry on.

Manager Shall I hold the lift for you, Mr Willey?

Richard No, I always use the stairs. Good for the figure.

Manager Quite.

The Manager pats his tummy and exits, leaving the hall door open

Richard moves to the door and watches the Manager disappear down the corridor. He then closes the door, throws his briefcase behind the divan and opens the bedroom door

Richard (*gleefully*) All clear, Miss Worthington.

Jane appears at the bedroom door wearing a dress and carrying her shoes; one in each hand

Jane You don't think the Manager will be popping in and out all evening, do you?

Richard goes to hold her hands but grasps the shoes

Richard Of course not. Why haven't you changed into your nightie?
Jane I've been too busy listening at the door.
Richard Well, hurry up, you beautiful creature!

Jane exits into the bedroom

Richard is left holding Jane's shoes. He puts the shoes on the chair and then can't resist a look into the bedroom

(*Calling*) Would you like me to help you out of your dress?
Jane (*off*) No, thank you!

Richard watches for a brief moment

Richard Are you sure? (*He starts to move into the bedroom*)
Jane (*off*) Get out!

Jane's dress comes flying through the open doorway and Richard catches it. He has one more peek into the bedroom

Richard Oo! (*He then hurries to the telephone, throwing the dress on the divan. He lifts the receiver and dials a London number. On the phone*) House of Commons? It's Richard Willey here. Put me through to my Parliamentary Private Secretary, please. ... George, it's Mr Willey. ... It's no concern of yours where I am. How's the debate going? ... (*Displeased*) Oh! Well, listen, I don't want to be disturbed unless it starts turning into a disaster. ... George! Put it this way, if the Prime Minister says "Where's that idiot Richard Willey?" you can contact me. ... No, I'm not at home—and don't ring there whatever you do! The number here is zero-seven-one eight-three-nine five-zero-nine-seven and I'm in room six-four-eight. ... No it's not a hotel, it's the Reading Room of the British Museum ... Stop asking questions, George, you're my PPS, just do as you're told! (*He puts the phone down and hurries to the radio. He switches it on and starts to look for some suitable music*)
Voice (*on the radio*) "... the Chancellor of the Exchequer said today that inflation will drop to below six per cent by next March ..."
Richard Bloody liar. (*He fiddles some more and finds some military band music*)

Jane comes out of the bedroom wearing a flimsy nightie

Jane (*referring to the music*) I think that might give us hiccups, Mr Willey.

Richard turns

Richard (*sexily*) Oh, you look gorgeous.
Jane Thank you, Minister.

Richard switches off the radio and moves to her

Richard Absolutely gorgeous!

He goes to embrace her but she speaks

Jane You know—this feels really naughty, Mr Willey.
Richard So it should, it is naughty. Do you mind if I slip into something more comfortable?

Richard picks up his case and goes into the bedroom

Jane (*calling*) I mean you're a Junior Minister and I'm one of the secretaries over there.

Richard appears, taking off his jacket

Richard Very democratic, though. Especially as the Prime Minister's *my* boss and the Leader of the Opposition is *your* boss.

Richard exits into the bedroom

Jane (*chuckling; calling*) My boss would hit the roof if he knew.

Richard enters, putting on his dressing gown

Richard My boss would go *through* it. (*He goes to kiss Jane*)
Jane I don't make a practice of doing this, Mr Willey.
Richard Quite right! Neither do I. (*He goes to kiss her again*)
Jane Come off it, Mr Willey.
Richard (*hurt*) Jane!
Jane You should hear the jokes about you that go around the typists' pool.
Richard (*surprised*) About me?
Jane About *you*, Mr Willey. And with a name like that some of the jokes are pretty strong, I can tell you.
Richard Disgraceful.

Jane laughs and sits on the divan

Jane I'm only teasing you, Mr Willey.
Richard Are you?
Jane (*teasing him*) Don't you like to be teased, Mr Willey?
Richard Depends what you mean by—"teased". And I wish you'd stop calling me "Mr Willey". (*He sits beside Jane*)
Jane I've never called you anything else.
Richard Well, under the circumstances I think you can call me—Dickie.
Jane (*giggling*) No, I couldn't.
Richard All my friends call me Dickie.

Jane No I couldn't. Not after all those jokes I've heard. I'll call you Richard.

Richard Coming from you, it sounds beautiful. Now, I've laid on some champagne.

Jane Lovely!

Richard Some caviare.

Jane Lovely!

Richard And three dozen oysters.

Jane Oysters! Aren't they supposed to do something to a chap? (*She rises and moves to the radio*)

Richard God, I hope so, they're damned expensive. What time do you have to be home in—er—where is it? Lewisham?

Jane I don't. I can stay all night.

Richard (*delighted*) All night! What have you told your husband then?

Jane I'm visiting Auntie Rosie in Felixstowe.

Jane presses a button on the radio, and the intro music of "Love And Marriage" is heard

Richard (*delighted*) Auntie Rosie in Felixstowe.

Jane She's developed severe bronchitis.

Richard Poor Auntie Rosie.

Jane And Auntie Rosie's not on the phone so—

Richard So your husband can't ring up to disturb you. Lovely!

He goes to kiss her as Frank Sinatra starts singing "Love And Marriage"

Richard There must be a more suitable song than that. (*He starts to fiddle with the radio*)

Jane It's a beautiful warm night. Shall I open the curtains? (*She moves to the window*)

Richard Why not? If I remember correctly there's a beautiful view. These balconies overlook the river.

Jane pulls the cord to open the curtains. The curtains open to reveal the body of a man in a raincoat. The window has come down on his neck. His head, shoulders and dangling arms are protruding into the room with the rest of his body in a prostrate position outside the balcony. Jane steps back to look out of the window and sees the Body. She emits no sound but her hands come up to her mouth and she staggers back a pace. She then turns from the window

Jane Ohhh!

Richard is still concentrating on the radio

Richard Breathtaking view, isn't it? Nelson's column one way. Big Ben the other.

Jane (*finally, trying to be calm*) Mr Willey——

Richard I've told you, "Dickie".

Jane I think I feel sick.

The radio starts to play some soft music

Richard (*going to her*) Can't stand heights, eh?
Jane (*grabbing Richard*) Oh, my God!
Richard Well, six floors is pretty high.
Jane Mr Willey——!
Richard (*holding up a remonstrative finger*) Dickie!
Jane Dickie! (*She moves past Richard*)
Richard (*going to the window*) Well, don't look down, just look up at ... (*He sees the Body*) Good god!

He kneels down to look at the man's face

(*Turning to Jane*) I think we can dispense with the background music.

Jane turns off the radio. She then moves to Richard who is feeling the man's pulse

The window must have come down on his neck.
Jane Oh, Mr Willey.
Richard I can't feel any pulse.
Jane He's dead, is he?
Richard (*tersely*) That's what "no pulse" usually means.

Jane kneels beside Richard

Jane How long's he been there?
Richard (*tetchily*) How do *I* know? The curtains were already closed when I arrived. I've been here about ten minutes.
Jane Is he still warm, Mr Willey?

Richard rises and backs away a pace

Richard Yes, he's still warm, Miss Worthington!
Jane (*rising*) He looks awful.
Richard 'Course he does, he's dead!
Jane Poor man.
Richard Poor man? He's obviously a burglar.
Jane Is he?
Richard Well, he's not the waiter delivering oysters, is he? Besides, we're six floors up. Of course he's a burglar.
Jane He might be one of the guests.
Richard Jane, it doesn't matter who he is, he was clearly breaking and entering. He must have somehow got on to our balcony (*he looks out of the window*)—it goes all round the hotel—forced the window open and— (*he mimes the window coming down*)—bang!
Jane Must be a dodgy sash or something.
Richard Well, he won't be suing the hotel, that's for sure.

Richard pulls the cord and closes the curtains. Jane picks up the telephone

Jane We'd better ring the police.
Richard Police?
Jane About him.
Richard We can't ring the police! (*He replaces the receiver*)

Jane We must, Mr Willey.

Richard How do we explain what you and I are doing in a suite at the *Westminster Hotel*? I'm supposed to be attending an all-night sitting in the House of Commons.

Jane But he's *dead*, Mr Willey.

Richard Well, the police won't be able to bring him round, will they? (*Suddenly, realizing*) God! If the P.M. finds out—! One more scandal for the Conservatives and we'll fall below the Liberal Democrats in the opinion polls.

Jane You can't discover a dead body and just ignore it. If you're worried about the police, phone down for the Manager.

Richard What's the difference? Look, Jane, I'm thinking about you.

Jane You're thinking about your wife, the Prime Minister and your career.

Richard Well those too. (*Suddenly*) God, I can see the headlines in *The Sun* now—Junior Minister and Labour Leader's secretary in sex-orgy with dead body.

Jane You've got to inform somebody!

Richard You're right. I'll inform George.

He goes to the phone

Jane Mr Pigden?

Richard (*dialling*) Yes.

Jane What will your PPS do?

Richard Whatever I tell him. (*On the phone*) Richard Willey here. Put me through to my PPS. . . . George, get over here right away. . . . Never mind the debate, just get over here. . . . No, not the British Museum, the *Westminster Hotel*. . . . Never you mind. You can be here in two minutes. Suite six-four-eight and don't tell anyone where you're going. . . . Bring anything with you? Yes, your brains, George, your brains. (*He slams the phone down*)

There is a knock at the door. They both hesitate

(*Calling; sweetly*) who is it?

Waiter (*off*) Room Service.

Richard (*calling*) I'm busy.

Jane You ordered champagne, caviare and oysters.

Richard I know!

Waiter (*off*) Room Service six-four-eight!

Richard Go away!

The Waiter knocks persistently

Waiter (*off*) Room Service! Six-four-eight.

Richard God, he'll have the whole hotel in here. Wait in the bedroom.

Jane But Mr Willey——

He pushes a protesting Jane into the bedroom

There is more knocking from outside. Richard sees Jane's shoes on the chair and quickly throws them into the bedroom, closing the door

Waiter (*off*) Room Service. Six-four-eight.
Richard Coming!

Richard quickly checks that the curtains are covering the Body then opens the door

   The Waiter comes in, pushing a trolley, and glares at Richard

Waiter If this was hot it would be cold.
Richard Just leave it there.

The Waiter pushes the trolley DL. *Richard sees Jane's dress, picks it up and starts to move to the bedroom*

Waiter Hey! You've got to sign.
Richard (*stopping*) All right!

The Waiter goes to his side pocket but his pad isn't there

Waiter I've got it here somewhere.
Richard Good!

The phone rings, Richard hesitates. The Waiter indicates that the phone is ringing. Richard angrily picks it up

   (*On the phone; sweetly*) Yes? (*Sweetly*) Mr Willey speaking. . . . (*Sweetly*) Oh, and what can I do for the Manager of this delightful hotel?

During the above the Waiter has found his pad in his back pocket and offers it to Richard to sign. Richard has the phone in one hand and the dress in the other, so he gives the dress to the Waiter to hold while he signs. Richard is just about to sign when he stops

   (*On the phone; alert*) Seen a what? . . . (*Flatly*) An intruder? . . . on our—er—

Richard looks at the closed curtains. So does the Waiter

   (*On the phone*) No, no. Nothing untoward at all . . . must have been somebody else's balcony. . . . No, there's no need to come up . . . our curtains are wide open, I can see there's nobody there.

The Waiter turns to look at the closed curtains

   (*On the phone*) I'm just about to leave for the Commons. . . . No, there's no need to put yourself out . . . There's obviously been a mistake. It must be some other balcony. . . . No, please. (*To the Waiter*) Go away! (*On the phone*) No, not you. . . . Hello. . . . Hello!

The Manager has rung off. Richard slams down the phone. He turns to see the Waiter who is now walking up to look at the window

   (*Yelling*) Hey!
Waiter (*jumping*) Ahhh!
Richard I'll sign that now.

Richard signs and at the same time leads the Waiter to the door

Thank you.

The Waiter hesitates, coughs and surreptitiously holds out his hand. Richard goes to his pocket and takes out his money clip. He gives the Waiter a five pound note and bundles him out. Neither he nor Richard notices that the Waiter is still carrying Jane's dress

Waiter (*impressed with the tip*) Thank you.

The Waiter exits

Richard slams the door and hurries to the window. He pulls the cord and the curtains open to reveal the Body still in place. Richard looks around quickly and then opens the cupboard door. The cupboard is shallow with a hook on the inside of the door, and a clothes rail—with hangers—in the cupboard. He pushes the window up and heaves the Body in. We now see that the Body is that of a short middle-aged man. Richard is holding the Body "face to face" when—

Jane comes in from the bedroom. She is carrying her bag, and wearing bra and pants

Jane Hey, you've got my . . .

She sees Richard with the Body and screams

Richard (*jumping*) Ahh!
Jane (*horrified*) What are you doing, Mr Willey?
Richard (*through gritted teeth*) The fox trot. What does it look like I'm doing, Miss Worthington!

The window behind them suddenly falls with a loud bang

(*Reacting to the window falling*) Ahh! Well, we can see how it happened now.

Richard starts to drag the Body to the cupboard

Jane You can't move him, Mr Willey!
Richard It won't make any difference to our friend here where he's discovered or who discovers him or when! I'll sort it out with George as soon as he arrives.
Jane This isn't right, Mr Willey.
Richard It's not supposed to be right. It's supposed to be expedient.

During the above dialogue Richard hangs the Body on the hook on the inside of the cupboard door. Jane looks horrified as Richard closes the door

Now you get home to Lewisham as fast as . . . (*He stops*) Why haven't you put your dress on?
Jane You've got it in here.
Richard No, I haven't. I threw it into the bedroom.
Jane You threw my shoes in.
Richard I gave your dress—(*realizing*)—to the waiter!

Jane The waiter!

There is a knock at the door. They look at each other

Richard (*calling; sweetly*) Who is it?
Manager (*off*) The Manager.
Richard Quick!

Richard starts to push Jane towards the bedroom

Jane (*whispering urgently*) Mr Willey, what are you doing?
Richard (*whispering urgently*) Ssh! In the bedroom.
Jane What about my dress?

Richard pushes Jane into the bedroom

Manager (*off*) Mr Willey!
Richard (*calling*) Coming!

Richard realizes he's wearing his dressing gown. He opens the bedroom door

(*Calling into the bedroom*) Throw me my jacket!

Jane enters, hands him his jacket and exits into the bedroom, closing the door

Richard, not realizing, puts the jacket on over his dressing gown

Manager (*off*) Mr Willey!
Richard (*calling*) Coming!

As Richard starts to move from the bedroom door, the cupboard door falls open and the Body appears still hanging on the hook

Oh, my God!

Richard hurries to the cupboard and closes the door

Manager (*off*) Mr Willey!
Richard (*calling; calmly*) Coming!

Richard does up the button on his jacket and opens the door

The Manager storms in, slamming the door behind him

Sorry about that.
Manager This is a very serious . . .

The Manager stops and reacts to Richard's attire

Richard Shall we go? I really must get back to the debate. (*Realizing*) Oh, silly me. (*He chuckles at the way he is dressed*)
Manager This is a very serious business, Mr Willey.

The Manager goes to the window, opens it, looks out and leans back in again. Richard gently moves the Manager down into the room. During the ensuing dialogue Richard removes his dressing gown and puts his jacket on properly

Richard Yes, I'm sorry I can't be of more assistance. It's been very quiet here actually.

Manager A guest nearby said she'd seen a man kneeling on this balcony looking through the window.

Richard Must be mistaken.

Manager No, this is the balcony all right. Suite six-four-eight. She said she'd watched this man for a good ten minutes. He didn't move a muscle. He just knelt outside—staring in.

Richard Good Lord! Well, as you can see, there's nobody there now. Let's forget all about it.

Manager Sounds like a Peeping Tom to me or, even worse, a burglar. I'll just go into your bedroom.

Richard Bedroom?

Manager The balcony goes past there too. Can't do any harm to check.

Suddenly the window falls with a loud bang. Richard jumps and clutches the Manager

I must tell maintenance about that. Excuse me.

As the Manager starts to move to the bedroom door Richard quickly opens it

Richard Allow me.

Manager I'll do it, Mr Willey.

Richard All right. Yes. (*Loudly for Jane's benefit*) It's a good idea for the Manager to check the bedroom window! (*He smiles at the Manager*)

Manager (*surprised by the shouting*) Thank you.

The Manager moves to go past Richard but Richard stops him

Richard And for the *Manager* to check the bedroom balcony!

Manager (*surprised*) Thank you.

The Manager moves to go past Richard. Again he stops him

Richard After the *Manager*! (*He hands the bewildered Manager his dressing gown*) Thank you.

Richard allows the bemused Manager to walk past him into the bedroom

There is a knock at the corridor door

(*Loudly, into the bedroom*) I'll just see who's at the door! (*He calls*) Who is it?

George (*off*) It's me, Mr Willey. George.

Richard opens the corridor door

George steps in, holding his briefcase

George I got here as fast as I——

Richard Shut up!

Richard pulls the surprised George into the room and shuts the door

Now, listen, Pigden. I'm going to say this once and very, very quickly. I discovered something extremely unpleasant in my suite tonight.

George When you say "sweet" do you mean pudding or——?

Richard (*interrupting*) Shut up! This body now resides in the coat cupboard.

George When you say body do you mean——?

Richard (*interrupting*) Shut up! We will arrange for this body to be discovered at some other place later tonight by your good self.

George I don't quite understand.

Richard (*pressing on*) By which time I will be in the House of Commons lending my support to the Transport Minister and the Leader of the Opposition's secretary will be tucked up in bed in Lewisham.

There is a pause as George attempts to take it all in

George Do you think I could go out and come in again?

Richard sits George in the chair R

Richard George! When the Hotel Manager comes out of that bedroom, remember—everything I've just told you *never happened.*

George goes to speak but then looks at Richard dumbly

There's been no intruder on the balcony. I've had a very quiet evening. There's no dead body in the coat cupboard.

George Well, thank goodness for small mer——

Richard Shut up! (*He continues*) *Nothing's happened.* Have you got that?

There is a moment's pause and then George shakes his head

For God's sake just agree with everything I say. Don't try to be helpful. Just look intelligent and nod your head.

George blankly nods his head

The Manager comes in from the bedroom

Manager Nothing unusual on that balcony either.

George rises but Richard sits him down immediately

Richard I thought not. Oh, this is my Parliamentary Private Secretary, Mr Pigden.

George gives a wan smile and nods intelligently

Yes. I'm afraid I've lumbered George with rather a lot of detailed work so I've asked him to stay in London overnight, haven't I, George?

George hesitates and then nods intelligently

Yes. So I was wondering if you could accommodate him.

Manager I'll see what I can do, Mr Willey.

Richard Actually—what would be perfect would be the suite next to this. Either side will do. Adjoining balconies. We need to be close, don't we, George?

George hesitates a little longer than usual but then nods intelligently

Manager I'll see if we have anything nearby, Mr Pigden.
Richard (*lightly*) Don't bother to get up, George.
Manager And I'll put our Security on to that intruder, Mr Willey.

The Manager moves to go. Richard leans nonchalantly against the cupboard door

Richard Oh, I wouldn't bother. There's been no damage. (*Intimately*) And not good publicity for the hotel, that kind of thing.
Manager Nevertheless, I have my . . . you're right, it's not good publicity, is it?
Richard Definitely not.
Manager Maybe it's a case of "least said, soonest mended".
Richard I'd like to borrow that phrase if I may.
Manager Thank you.

The Manager looks pleased and exits

George Mr Willey . . .?
Richard Well done, George. Every nod was a gem.
George What on earth's going on?!
Richard You're going to have a free overnight stay at a four star hotel.

Richard moves to the bedroom but George stops him

George I never stay out without telling Mother.

Richard grimaces

Richard Well give your mother a ring. She'll be thrilled for you.
George She's already in bed. Besides there's Nurse Foster.
Richard Nurse Foster?
George She looks after Mother while I'm at work. She goes off at nine-thirty.
Richard You can phone Nurse Foster and tell her she'll be doing some overtime.
George I never take advantage of her like that, Mr Willey. Anyway, Mother worries herself to death if I change my plans at the last minute.
Richard Your mother has been worrying herself to death for the last eighty years. The future of the Government is at stake here.
George But *why*?

By way of an explanation Richard quickly opens the bedroom door

Richard Quickly! Out you come, Miss Worthington.
George (*surprised and concerned*) Miss Worthington?

Jane appears still carrying her bag and still dressed in bra and pants

Jane Have you got my dress . . .? (*She sees George*) Oh, Mr Pigden. (*She moves to George*)
George (*mortified*) Miss Worthington!
Richard Now can you see the problem?

George goes to speak but decides to simply nod

Jane Good-evening, Mr Pigden.
George *(eyeing her bra)* Good-evening, Miss Worthingtons—Worthington. *(To Richard)* Mr Willey, how could you?!
Richard I haven't yet, George, but that's the least of my problems. First of all we've got to get Miss Worthington's dress back.
George Where is it for heaven's sake?
Richard I gave it to the waiter.
George Ask a silly question.
Jane *(to Richard)* What did you tell the Manager just now?
Richard Never mind. George is stepping into the breach.
George Not until he knows all the facts.
Jane *(to Richard)* Have you told Mr Pigden about the dead body?
Richard Yes, yes, yes.
George *(aghast)* You mean there *is* a dead body?! You said there wasn't.
Richard No, I didn't. I said to tell the *Manager* there wasn't.
George I can't follow this.
Richard All the Manager knows is that there's an intruder.
George Intruder?
Richard What the Manager doesn't know is that the intruder was a dead body.
George *(perplexed)* The intruder was a dead body?
Jane He was stuck in our window.
George The Manager or the intruder?
Richard The intruder!
Jane With his neck broken.
George Oh, I see. *(Realizing)* Neck broken?!

Richard opens the bedroom door

Richard Thank you, Miss Worthington! Will you kindly wait in the bedroom while I retrieve your dress.
Jane How will I know when it is safe to come out?
Richard I'll shout!
Jane I'm sorry you've got involved in this, Mr Pigden.
George That's all right.

Jane exits

(Rising) I'm not involved in it!

Richard sits him down and hurries to the phone

Richard I need your help like I've never needed it before, George. *(He dials Room Service)*
George *(rising concerned)* Wait a minute. When I arrived you told me the body was in that cupboard.
Richard It is. *(On the phone)* Hello! Are you the gentleman who's been providing six-four-eight with Room Service? . . . Good. You went off with a dress just now . . . I gave you a *dress*! *(To George)* Stupid man. *(On the phone)* I want it back . . . I want my dress back! Six-four-eight and *hurry*,

you silly old bat! (*He slams the phone down.* To George) Next time there's a debate on euthanasia I'm voting in favour.

George (*fearing the worst*) Mr Willey, could I return to the body in the cupboard?

Richard I knew you'd come to my aid, George.

George Oh, no! First of all I just want to know how it got from outside the window *there* to inside the cupboard *there*.

Richard I think you'd better sit down, George.

George (*understanding the situation*) Oh, no. Mr Willey! You didn't!

Richard sits George down

Richard (*pleading*) George! I had no alternative.

George (*mortified*) You didn't move a dead body?

Richard I had to think quickly. He's only a burglar for God's sake.

George (*in disbelief*) You haven't informed the police or anybody?

Richard No, that's why I need your help, George.

George (*determinedly*) I'm sorry, Mr Willey. (*He rises and moves away*)

Richard George! My wife thinks I'm in the House of Commons! It would all come out. Miss Worthington! The lot!

George Mr Willey—you have tampered with material evidence.

Richard My wife will tamper with something else if she finds out about Miss Worthington. George, you're not married. You don't know how terrifying an angry wife can be.

George If I was married, Mr Willey, I would be faithful to my wife!

Richard takes George's briefcase and sits him in the chair R

Richard That's because you're a far better person than I am, George. Now, all we have to do——

George (*rising*) There's no "we" about it.

Richard OK all "you" have to do——

George I don't have to do anything!

Richard As soon as the Manager finds you a room we transfer the body——

George We do what?!

Richard Transfer the body. To your suite. We'll arrange him on your window ledge and then—when I'm safely back in the House of Commons and Miss Worthington is in Lewisham—you will open your curtains, discover the poor unfortunate chap and report it immediately to the Manager.

George Just like that! Move the body to *my* suite. Lay him out on *my* window ledge. You and Miss Worthington—(*He mimes "leaving"*) Poor George Pigden—(*He mimes cutting his throat*)

Richard George, if you won't do it for *me* think of Miss Worthington! The poor girl's career will be ruined. She's the Labour Leader's secretary for God's sake.

George I've told you a hundred times where your libido would lead you.

Richard (*suddenly very moved*) You'd also be doing it for our Prime Minister. He'd have to ask me to resign. That'll be three in the last twelve months. George, the Government would never win the next election.

George hesitates

George It's in the cupboard, is it?
Richard Hanging on a hook.

*George grimaces. He hesitates a moment and then moves to the cupboard door.
He stops and looks at Richard*

You'll get a shock, George!

*George averting his eyes, opens the cupboard door. The Body is still hanging
on the inside of the door. Slowly George turns to look inside the cupboard. The
cupboard is empty. He starts to chuckle, believing that Richard has been
playing a joke on him. Still laughing, George sees the dead body hanging on the
inside of the door. For a moment he continues laughing but then suddenly stops
and screams*

   *The Manager enters from the hall without seeing George. He removes his
   pass key from the lock*

Manager (*as he enters*) Good news, Mr Willey!
George Ahhh!

*At the sound of the Manager's voice, George steps into the cupboard and closes
the door in one deft movement. Richard drops to his knees. The Manager
surveys Richard on the floor*

Richard (*rising*) That's a very good quality carpet you have there.
Manager (*ignoring Richard*) I've found Mr Pigden a suite which is—oh,
   where's Mr Pigden?
Richard He's in the loo.

Richard leads the Manager away from the cupboard

   (*Shouting across to the bedroom, for Jane's benefit*) I've told the *Manager*
   you're in the "loo"! (*He smiles at the surprised Manager*)
Manager I've managed to get him suite six-fifty.
Richard (*shouting*) The *Manager* says it's suite six-fifty.

The Manager is getting perplexed

Manager Right opposite.
Richard (*shouting*) The Manager says it's right opposite!

   Jane comes out of the bedroom still in her bra and pants

Jane OK, you don't have to shout as loud—oh!

*She stops on seeing the Manager. The Manager steps back a pace. There is a
pause as Richard and the surprised Manager take in the situation*

Richard This is Mrs Pigden.
Manager Mrs Pigden?!
Richard Didn't I tell you?
Manager No!

Richard Yes, his wife's staying up with him tonight. (*To Jane*) Aren't you, Mrs Pigden?
Jane Am I?
Richard Oh, yes, the Manager's fixed it. Suite six-fifty. Just across the corridor. (*To the Manager*) That was so kind.
Manager I thought Mr Pigden was staying up to assist you with your work.
Richard That's right but who am I to deny him a little pleasure with his business? (*Referring to Jane*) Can you blame him? (*Chuckling*) A delectable wife. A suite at the Westminster. All paid for by the government. George telephoned her and she was round here like a shot. Dropped everything.
Manager (*pointedly looking at Jane*) Yes.
Richard Now you're probably wondering why Mrs Pigden is wearing—er . . . (*He indicates her state of undress*)

The Manager says nothing

Yes. She was in the shower. Mr Pigden's in the loo. All nice and intimate. There you have it. (*To Jane*) I think that sums it up, doesn't it?
Jane I think so.
Richard (*to the Manager*) Yes, that's about the size of it.

The Maid knocks on the open door and enters

Maid 'Scusa, Signor.
Richard What is it?
Maid (*carefully*) Make—bed-up.
Richard (*indicating Jane*) No, we'll do it. (*Quickly*) I will do it.
Maid Oh, si. (*She sees Jane*) Oh, si! (*She giggles*)
Richard We're busy!
Maid (*not understanding*) Non capisco.
Richard Go. Bye-bye.
Maid Oh, go bye-bye. Si! (*She indicates Jane and giggles*)
Manager Thank you, Maria.
Maid Si.

The Maid curtsies and exits

Richard (*to the manager*) And thank you so much.
Manager Yes. (*To Jane*) Well, I'll have the key to six-fifty sent up. You can move in immediately, Mrs Pigden.
Richard Splendid.
Manager (*to Jane*) Or when you've completed your ablutions, that is. And then will either you or Mr Pigden be good enough to come down to Reception and check-in right away.
Richard No problem.

Richard leads the Manager towards the door

Manager And I thought you were in a hurry to get back to the House of Commons, Mr Willey.
Richard Yes, I'm on my way right now. I'm just waiting for the "loo".

The Manager gives Richard a blank look and moves to go. Behind them the cupboard door opens and, with one deft movement Richard bangs it shut

George (*yelling; off*) Oh!

The Manager looks at Richard

Richard Oh!

Richard crosses his legs and holds his stomach as though anxious to go to the toilet

The Manager looks at Richard and exits

Jane Mr Willey, what have you done?
Richard I thought I did very well, actually. (*He opens the cupboard door*) George!

George steps out of the cupboard. He realizes he is inadvertently holding the Body's hand

George Ahh! Oh, that was terrible.

There is a knock at the corridor door

  Ahh!

George goes to step back into the cupboard but Richard stops him and closes the cupboard door

Richard Who is it?
Waiter (*off*) Room Service.
Richard Great. (*To Jane*) Your dress.

Richard opens the door

  Quick!

The Waiter steps in and gives Richard a sheet of notepaper. Richard looks at it blankly

  (*To the Waiter*) What the hell's this?
Waiter You asked for my address.

Richard throws his hands in the air and walks away in disbelief

George Mr Willey wanted a *dress*.
Waiter (*looking at Richard; surprised*) Did he?
Jane It's dark blue with little flowers.
Waiter (*smiling at Richard*) Sounds nice.
Richard You took it!
Waiter (*remembering*) Oh, a *dress*.
Richard Yes!
Waiter I wondered how I came by that. You're right, I am a silly old bat.
Jane Will you go and get it, please.
Richard And hurry!

Waiter No sooner—Oh—the Manager said somebody here was checking in to suite six-fifty.
Richard That's correct, Mr and Mrs Pigden.

George looks around for "Mrs Pigden"

Waiter Mr and Mrs Pigden.
Richard Yes. Mr Pigden here. And Mrs Pigden there.

George looks again for "Mrs Pigden"

Jane Darling.

Jane puts her arm through George's and squeezes him lovingly. George looks at her and then can only nod

Waiter (*producing a key*) One key.

Richard takes the key

Richard (*handing the key to George*) There we are, George.
Waiter Do you have any bags, Mr Pigden?
George (*rubbing his eyes*) Not yet, no.
Richard No. No bags, no cases. Nothing like that. They're on their honeymoon.
George (*faintly*) Oh, my God! (*He sits in the chair* R)
Richard Yes. Married this morning. In Lewisham. Yes. Well, the hotel's my wedding present, George. (*He laughs gaily*) When I say "the hotel's my wedding present"—I mean, the suite, of course. Nice way to spend a honeymoon.
Waiter (*to George*) You're sure you want me to bother fetching your wife's dress?
George Yes, please!
Richard (*to the Waiter*) And we'd like it quickly.

The Waiter hesitates, holds out his hand and emits his cough. Richard gives him five pounds

Waiter Most kind. (*Referring to the trolley*) Oh, you haven't touched your supper.
Richard We don't want it, thank you.
Waiter But you've paid for it.
Richard Just take it away.
Waiter (*taking the trolley*) Right. I'll sell it to one of the other guests.

The Waiter exits

George Mr Willey, I wish to register my strong objection to all of this.
Richard Right, George, it's registered. Jane, wait in the bedroom. As soon as your dress arrives, go. (*He opens the bedroom door*)
Jane I'm so sorry about tonight, Mr Pigden.
Richard He's having a ball. (*He pushes Jane into the bedroom*) OK, George. Get yourself into suite six-fifty.

George Wait a minute! I've got to call Nurse Foster. (*He lifts the receiver and dials*)
Richard Nurse Foster?
George To tell her I'm going to be late.
Richard Well hurry up, for heaven's sake.
George The world doesn't totally revolve around you, Mr Willey.
Richard Never mind the sermon, George, just be quick about it.

Richard opens the cupboard door and the Body is revealed once more

George (*on the phone*) Hello, is that Miss Foster? ... Good-evening, it's Mr Pigden here. ... I'm fine, thank you. ... Yes, I'm keeping very fit, thank you.

Richard, who has turned from the cupboard, advances on George

Richard She doesn't need a medical report, George!
George (*on the phone*) How's Mother been today?
Richard God!
George (*on the phone*) Oh, dear. ... Oh dear, oh dear. (*To Richard*) Mother's been a wee bit restless.
Richard We're *all* restless, George! Tell the Nurse you're going to be late.
George (*on the phone*) I was wondering if I could ask a small favour. ... Thank you. (*To Richard*) She says nothing's too much trouble for me.
Richard Good. (*He moves up and opens the window*)
George (*on the phone*) I may be a little late tonight. Something's cropped up. ... That's very good of you, Miss Foster. ... Ah no! If Mother wants to call me she'll have to ring me on zero-seven-one eight-three-nine five-zero-nine-seven.
Richard George!
George I always like Mother to know where I am in case of emergencies. (*On the phone*) And I'll either be in room six-four-eight or six-fifty ... They're Reading Rooms in the British Museum ... Thank you so much. (*He puts the phone down*)
Richard Right, George. Get into suite six-fifty there, open the window and then come back in here via the balcony.
George I suffer from vertigo, you know.
Richard Good, that'll take your mind off the corpse you'll be carrying.

Richard pushes George into the corridor. George starts to unlock 650 door

Richard closes the door and then goes to the Body as:

Jane comes in from the bedroom

Jane Mr Willey!
Richard Ahhh! Don't *do* that, Miss Worthington.
Jane I've just realized, I've nowhere to go.
Richard What do you mean? As soon as you're dressed, go home.
Jane I can't. My husband thinks I'm with Auntie Rosie in Felixstowe.
Richard Well go to Auntie Rosie in Felixstowe! (*He looks out of the window UL for George*)

Jane She'd have a fit if I turn up in the early hours of the morning.
Richard (*turning to Jane*) Then bed down with Pigden in suite six-fifty.

George appears at the window from UL

George I heard that, Mr Willey.
Richard Quick, George, I'll give you a hand. (*He goes to lift the Body off the hook*)
George I've been having second thoughts about the whole thing.

The Manager enters

Richard steps into the cupboard and Jane closes the door on him and the Body

The Manager removes his pass key from the lock

Manager (*as he enters*) I can't find Mr or Mrs Pigden in their——

He stops on seeing George kneeling outside the window. George smiles at the Manager and gives a friendly wave. The Manager advances on George who continues to smile happily and tries to look nonchalant

(*Finally*) What are you doing out there, Mr Pigden?
George Coming in.

Before George can move, the window descends with a loud bang in front of his face. The Manager opens it

Manager I've just been into suite six-fifty looking for you and Mrs Pigden.
George I came over to admire the view. It's great in here. (*To Jane*) Come on, darling, I'll take you back. (*He offers his hand*)
Jane (*to the Manager*) Excuse me.

She climbs out through the window and follows George off UL

George (*as he goes*) Bye-bye.
Manager (*calling*) And then will you kindly check-in at Reception immediately.

Richard comes out of the cupboard

George (*off*) Of course!
Richard (*to the Manager*) Crazy honeymooners.

The Manager turns to see Richard standing beside him

Manager (*calmly*) You're missing your debate, Mr Willey.
Richard I just need to go to the loo first.

Richard crosses his legs and moves towards the bedroom door. Richard stops when he realizes that the Manager, instead of leaving, is watching him

After you.

Richard indicates for the Manager to leave. The Manager moves. The window falls with a bang

(*Jumping*) Ahhh!

The Manager returns and looks enquiringly at Richard, waiting for him to speak

Richard Ahhh.

Richard indicates the urgency of going to the toilet. The manager nods and moves to go as the cupboard door swings open and the Body is revealed

(*Inadvertently yelling*) Ahhh!

The Manager stops and turns to look at Richard, who indicates that the necessity to go to the toilet is getting more urgent

The Manager never taking his eyes off Richard, and so still not seeing the Body, exits, closing the door

Richard hurries to the window and opens it

(*Calling off* UL) George! (*He shuts the cupboard door and returns to the window. Calling*) George! (*He climbs out on to the balcony*) George!

Richard exits along the balcony UL

There is a knock at the corridor door

After a moment, the Waiter enters holding out the dress

Waiter Here we are—! Hello! Room Service!

The Waiter hesitates and starts to go. The phone rings. The Waiter hesitates and then lifts the receiver

(*On the phone*) Hello? . . . Yes. this is six-four-eight. . . . No it's not one of the Reading Rooms at the British Museum. . . . Yes, the telephone number here is zero-seven-one eight-three-nine five-zero-nine-seven but it's the *Westminster Hotel* . . . Madam, I'd *know* if I worked in the British Museum. . . . Mr George Pigden? Yes, I know Mr Pigden. . . . Message from who. . . . Nurse Foster? And what's the message Nurse Foster? . . . His mother's a bit worried about tonight and wants to talk to him. . . . Well, you tell Mrs Pigden there's no cause to worry. Her son's honeymoon is going like a bomb.

He puts down the phone and exits happily into the corridor, closing the door

Richard, George and Jane appear outside the window from UL

Richard Come on.

The three of them enter through the window

Jane, you guard the hall door. George and I will transport the cause of all our problems to six-fifty.

Jane goes to the corridor door while Richard and George get the Body off the hook. Jane closes the cupboard door

George Oh dear! I hope my mother doesn't start worrying about me.
Richard Forget your mother for five minutes! Come on George. Don't hang about.

As they turn to the window the Waiter appears on the balcony from UL *still carrying the dress*

Waiter I say!

In one deft movement George and Richard straighten up with the Body between them. They have the Body's arms around their shoulders supporting him, and the three of them are standing in a row

The Waiter steps over the window ledge, into the room as:

George and Richard move quickly away in front of the divan with the Body between them. The Waiter moves down and surveys the tableau. By way of explanation George and Richard start "dancing" and singing with the Body between them. The Waiter is mesmerized. They finish their brief but bright routine and Jane, who has come DL *to watch, applauds*

Richard Thank you, Mrs Pigden. (*To George*) A little more practice, George, and it will be ready for the Conservative Conference Cabaret.

The window suddenly falls with a bang. George and Richard yell. George and the Body collapse on to the divan

Quite right, George. You and your *brother* take a rest.
George Oh, my God!
Richard (*lightly*) Is Fred worn out, George?
George Dead beat.
Richard Your brother's not got your stamina, George. (*To the Waiter*) Fred was George's best man at the wedding this morning. I think he's had a few too many. Pull yourself together, Fred!

Richard slaps Fred on the shoulder. The Body flops forward. George pulls it back

You'll be all right, Fred. (*To the Waiter*) So, what's your problem?
Waiter (*bemused*) What? Oh. Yes. I've got your dress.

During the ensuing dialogue Richard takes the dress from the Waiter, tips him a five pound note and leads him to the door. Jane moves up and opens the door

Richard Thank you. Most kind. If you can be of any further service tonight we won't hesitate to ring through and ask for you, personally. What's your name by the way?
Waiter (*looking at George and the Body*) Cromwell.
Richard Cromwell, eh? What's your first name, Oliver?

Richard chuckles but the Waiter is still mesmerized by George and the Body

Waiter No. Harold.
Richard (*giving him five pounds*) Well, you buy yourself a little something, Harold.
Waiter (*still looking at George*) Thank you.

Richard gives the Waiter another five pounds

Richard Open a small guest house somewhere.

Richard turns the Waiter round and gently pushes him out of the room closing the door

George rises and steps away from the Body, which slumps on to the divan

George (*in anguish*) Oh, my God!
Richard (*handing Jane the dress*) Quick, put this on, then go down to Reception and check-in as Mr and Mrs Pigden before the Manager blows his top.

During the next few lines Jane very quickly slips into her dress. Richard takes a pair of sun-glasses from his jacket pocket

George, stick my sun-glasses on him, he'll look better.

George takes the sun-glasses

George Oh, my goodness! (*He starts to put the sun-glasses on the Body*)
Richard (*to Jane*) After you've checked-in go home to Lewisham. George and I will get him into six-fifty.

The telephone rings. They all freeze. Richard lifts the receiver

Richard (*on the phone; brightly*) Hello? . . . (*Tersely*) Nurse Foster?!
George Nurse Foster?
Richard Ssh! (*On the phone*) No, you can't talk to Mr Pigden.
George Is Mother all right?
Richard Ssh! (*On the phone*) Mr Pigden has his hands full at the moment. . . . I'm the Curator at the British Museum . . . I'm the Curator at the British Museum and I'm staying overnight at the *Westminster Hotel*. . . . Oh! . . . Ah! . . . I see!
George What's she saying?
Richard Ssh! (*On the phone*) I'll get Mr Pigden to ring you back. (*He replaces the receiver*)
George What's happened?
Richard That was Nurse Foster. Your mother's upset about you being late home.
George Is that all?
Richard Not quite. She's even more upset that you got married today without telling her.
George Married?! (*He rises and the Body slumps on to the settee*)
Jane How on earth did she hear about that?
George My poor mother.
Richard Never mind your mother. Let's deal with the body and Miss Worthington.

As Richard takes hold of Jane:

The Manager appears outside the open window

Manager There you are!

Richard grabs Jane and calmly waltzes her around the room. George quickly sits beside the body back on the divan and holds it with his arm around its shoulders

The Manager comes through the open window and glares at the cavorting Richard. He taps Richard on the shoulder

Richard I'm afraid it's not an "Excuse me". (*He continues to dance with Jane. Singing*) "La Donna é Mobile". It's been one helluva day.

Richard opens the door and ushers Jane out into the corridor

Jane, still dancing, exits

(*To the Manager*) Rehearsing for the Conservative Conference Cabaret. Mrs Pigden is just going down to Reception to book in. Sorry about the delay.

Manager Thank you! Now. Mr Pigden —

The Manager turns and for the first time sees George sitting with the Body beside him

Who on earth is that?

Richard That's Mr Pigden's brother, Fred.

Manager (*looking at George*) Brother?

George Fred's not staying.

Manager Is your brother all right, Mr Pigden?

George Oh, he's fine. (*To the Body*) Aren't you, Fred? (*To the Manager*) Fine. (*He cuddles the Body*)

Richard Fred's just had a few too many drinks.

Manager Well, I suppose we could find a room for him here, Mr Pigden.

George Oh, no. Fred's got to get home. He's got a hell of a journey.

Manager He doesn't look too good.

George Oh, he always looks a bit pasty. Don't you, Fred?

George manipulates the Body so that it gesticulates a broad gesture with one of its arms

Manager (*to the Body*) Are you sure you feel up to it, Mr Pigden? (*He sits down next to George*)

George averts the Body's head

(*Calling across George*) Mr Pigden.

Richard He's rather deaf.

Manager (*louder*) Are you sure you feel up to it, Mr Pigden?

George, holding the back of the Body's head, turns its face to look at them. George grimaces at finding the Body's face so close to his

(*Loudly*) It would be no trouble to find you a room.

There is a slight pause and then the Body slowly shakes his head

(*Loudly*) Are you in a fit condition to get home?

The Body nods its head

I hope he's not driving, that's all.

Richard I'm pretty sure he won't be driving. Keep death off the road.

Manager (*to the Body*) Good-evening then, Mr Pigden.

The Body "waves" good-bye

The bemused Manager waves and exits

Richard You were brilliant, George.

George I feel sick.

Richard Come on, let's get him next door.

George It's no good getting him next door now!

Richard Why not?

George Why not?!

George rises and the Body falls behind the divan with a thump. George and Richard react

I'll tell you "why not", Mr Willey. Because the Manager has just spent five minutes talking to him and he thinks he's my brother, Fred! (*He holds his head in his hands and walks away in agony*)

Richard (*realizing*) You're right, George!

George (*moaning*) Why. Why did I listen to you?!

Richard George, we've got to think clearly.

George You can forget the royal "we" now.

Richard George, you're in this as much as I am. Who was doing the ventriloquist act with the dead body just now?

George (*trying to think*) Yes, well—

Richard And who's gone along with all this stuff about Mrs Pigden and the honeymoon?

George Yes, well—

Richard And tipsy brother Fred.

George I'll tell you one thing. I'm voting Labour next time.

Richard Right! Now the problem is—the Manager saw your brother Fred wearing a raincoat, scarf, suit, brown shoes, etc. and sporting sun-glasses.

George That's right!

Richard Well, if he *wasn't* wearing a raincoat, scarf, suit, brown shoes, etc. and sporting sun-glasses, but wearing something entirely *different*—I don't think he'd be recognized as your brother, Fred.

George (*aghast*) We can't strip a dead body, Mr Willey.

Richard This is no time to be squeamish, George. Get him back into the cupboard for the moment. (*He moves to the telephone*)

George What are you doing?

Richard (*dialling*) Phoning Oliver Cromwell.

George Who?

Richard Harold, or whatever his name is. (*On the phone*) Is that my old friend, Harold? ... Good. It's Mr Willey here. ... Yes, that's right, the rich gentleman in six-four-eight ...

During the ensuing dialogue George starts to drag the Body towards the cupboard but stops, getting caught up in Richard's conversation

Now, Harold, a little favour. . . . Yes, there's plenty more where the other came from! Do you have a change of clothes in the hotel? Jacket, trousers, shoes, that kind of thing. . . . Excellent. Bring them to suite six-four-eight right away. . . . We're collecting for Oxfam. (*He puts the phone down*)

There is urgent knocking at the door. George freezes with the Body

(*Sweetly*) Who is it?
Jane (*off*) Me, Jane. Quick, open the door.

Richard opens the door

Jane enters looking distraught

Richard Why haven't you left?
Jane Because I saw Ronnie at Reception.
Richard Ronnie? Who's Ronnie?
Jane My husband!

There is a brief pause as Richard and George take this in

George ⎰ (*together*) Husband?!
Richard ⎱
Richard (*aghast*) Ronnie's in Lewisham.
Jane Ronnie's at Reception.
George (*moaning*) Ohhh.

George sinks to his knees in despair, the Body sinking with him

Richard He can't be.
Jane He is. I got the shock of my life. Thank heavens *he* didn't see *me*.
Richard What the hell's he doing in the *Westminster Hotel*?
Jane I don't know.
George I knew something like this——
Richard (*interrupting*) Oh, shut up, George! And get off your knees, it's no good you and your brother praying.
George I think that's all that's left.

The phone rings. They freeze. Richard lifts the receiver

Richard (*on the phone; brightly*) Hello! . . . (*Angrily*) Not again, Nurse Foster!
George I'll talk to her!

George stands up and the Body sinks to its knees with its head resting on the chair

Richard You look after *him*. (*On the phone*) Miss Foster, you really must stop pestering Mr Pigden . . . Mr Pigden's mother is always having hysterics.
George What's happened?
Richard Nothing. (*On the phone*) What? . . . It's no concern of yours or Mrs Pigden's who George got married to today.
George Oh, my God! (*He hurries to Richard*)

Richard (*on the phone*) Mr Pigden will be home as soon as he's completed his marital duties. (*He slams down the phone*)

George My mother's probably having a heart attack.

Richard Well, let's hope that keeps Nurse Foster off the phone for five minutes.

Richard pushes George back to the Body

Now stop moaning and hang Fred on his hook!

George (*lifting the Body*) Come on, Fred!

George "marches" the Body to the cupboard

Jane What about Ronnie, Mr Willey?!

Richard Don't let's panic. There's obviously a perfectly simple explanation for Mr Worthington's unexpected arrival.

There's a knock on the corridor door. They all freeze. George has just got the Body back on its hook

(*Sweetly*) Who is it?

Ronnie (*off*) Open the door!

Jane (*horrified*) It's Ronnie.

George Oh, my God!

George steps into the cupboard. Richard pulls George out again

Richard (*sweetly*) Is that Room Service?

Ronnie If you don't open this door, I'll kick it in.

Richard (*whispering urgently*) Get Miss Worthington into suite six-fifty.

George (*whispering fiercely*) That's the best idea you've had tonight. (*He starts to climb on to the balcony*)

Jane He's got a terrible temper, Mr Willey.

Richard (*worried*) Has he?

George Mr Willey can handle it, come on.

George pulls Jane out through the window and they exit

There is a knocking at the corridor door

Ronnie (*off*) Hey!

Richard (*sweetly*) Coming!

Without having time to close the window Richard moves to the door. He pulls himself together, and then opens it

Ronnie marches in past Richard. He is in a high state of agitation

Richard (*pleasantly*) Oh. I thought you were the waiter.

Ronnie (*grimly*) I'm Ronnie Worthington.

Richard (*pleasantly*) Pleasure to meet you, Ronnie.

Richard offers his hand which Ronnie ignores

I'm Richard Willey.

Ronnie I bloody know who you are all right.
Richard (*smiling*) Yes, that's what comes of having the TV cameras in the House of Commons. You're—er—you're not one of my constituents, are you?
Ronnie No, I'm bloody not.

Ronnie opens the bedroom door and goes in

Richard (*calling through*) Ah. I thought that's maybe why you wanted to see me.

Ronnie comes back

Ronnie I'm Jane's husband.
Richard (*lightly*) Jane?
Ronnie Jane Worthington! (*He bangs the bedroom door shut*)
Richard (*lightly*) Jane Worthington?
Ronnie She's one of the secretaries over there!
Richard (*thinking; lightly*) No, I can't say I remember her.
Ronnie Look, you can drop all this. Where is she?
Richard Where's who?
Ronnie My wife! Miss Worthington.
Richard Ah, Miss Worthington is your wife. Miss as in "Ms".

Richard chuckles. Ronnie refrains

Ronnie Where is she?
Richard (*lightly dismissive*) Now what would a female secretary be doing in the hotel suite of a Junior Government Minister?
Ronnie It's no good, Mr Willey, I've had her followed.

Suddenly the window behind them descends with a bang. Richard gives a definite but contained reaction. Ronnie just looks at the window and backs to Richard

Richard Followed?
Ronnie Little tête-a-têtes. Corner cafes. Cups of tea—
Richard Oh, *that* Miss Worthington! Of course. *Jane!* One of the secretaries.—(*He laughs*) Dear Jane.
Ronnie I know what you've been up to!
Richard Shorthand, dictation—
Ronnie Come off it! You're a Conservative. She's in Labour.

Richard chuckles at Ronnie but the pun is lost on him

So when Jane started giving me all this rubbish about seeing her Auntie Rosie in Felixstowe!
Richard If you're suggesting what I think you're suggesting.
Ronnie I'm suggesting that to get to Felixstowe you don't have to change at the *Westminster Hotel!*

Richard digests this

The Maid knocks and enters

Maid Made-bed-now.
Ronnie (*advancing on the Maid*) There's no bloody beds going to be made tonight.
Maid Non capisco.
Ronnie Push off!
Maid (*pleasantly*) Bye-bye.

The Maid exits

Richard Now, my dear young man—
Ronnie Don't you "dear young man" me. When you were booking in, Mr Baker was standing right beside you.
Richard Mr Baker?
Ronnie My Private Detective.
Richard (*trying to smile*) Private Detective?
Ronnie And while I was waiting over the road Mr Baker clambered up the fire-escape——

An unpleasant thought formulates in Richard's mind and he looks towards the window

—got through the window of six-four-eight—and was arranging to catch you at it, my old chum!
Richard While I was booking in—your Private Detective came up the fire-escape—
Ronnie That's right!

Richard looks at the window

Richard And opened that window—
Ronnie You've hit it right on the head!
Richard Oh dear. (*He glances at the cupboard then back to Ronnie and smiles*)
Ronnie Yes! Well I've been waiting for him for over forty-five minutes so I reckon he must have seen plenty by now.
Richard You don't even know your wife's in the hotel.
Ronnie Yes I do. I've been standing opposite! I saw her sneak through after you'd checked-in.
Richard Possibly you did.
Ronnie *Definitely* I did!
Richard Well, she's not with me I assure you.

There is a fractional pause

She's with George Pigden.
Ronnie George who?
Richard George Pigden. I've been trying to protect him. He's my Private Secretary. Biggest ram in Westminster.
Ronnie Don't give me that. You're the one Jane's been having all those private meetings with.

Richard That's right. To try to talk her out of her infatuation for Mr Pigden. But it was to no avail. George is a very experienced womanizer. He's been through the female members over there like a sex-mad rabbit.

Ronnie What do you take me for?

Richard takes Ronnie to the door

Richard A very intelligent man, Ronnie. You go down to Reception. Check if there's a Mr and Mrs Pigden booked in.

Ronnie (*hesitating*) Look, if you're having me on.

Richard I'm as distressed as you are.

Richard opens the corridor door as, behind Ronnie, the cupboard door opens and the Body falls forward hanging on the hook. Richard sees this but Ronnie doesn't. Richard grabs Ronnie's shoulders to stop him turning

Ronnie!

Ronnie (*surprised*) What?

Richard I think I'm even more distressed than you are.

Ronnie George Pigden, you say?

Richard Correct. (*Sympathetically*) I'm dreadfully sorry it's going on behind your back.

Ronnie If you're lying to me—

Richard (*hurt*) Ronnie, I'm a Member of Parliament.

Ronnie Well, don't forget there's still Jack Baker.

Richard I haven't forgotten Jack Baker.

Ronnie He'll have kept his eyes open.

Richard He won't be able to say a word against me, I assure you.

Ronnie I'll be back.

Richard The pleasure will be all mine.

Richard pushes Ronnie into the corridor making sure that Ronnie doesn't turn around

Richard quickly shuts the Body away in the cupboard, goes to the telephone and dials

(*To himself*) Come on, George! (*On the phone*) George, get back in here with Jane, right away ... Ronnie's gone down to Reception but he'll be back ... You can't stay in six-fifty, that's where he's going back to ... George, there isn't time! Suffice to say that if Ronnie meets you we'll have two dead bodies on our hands. (*He puts the phone down*)

There is a knock on the door

(*Sweetly*) Who is it?

Waiter (*off*) Room Service.

Richard opens the door

The Waiter enters carrying a pile of clothes on top of which is a bowler hat

Waiter Your bespoke tailor has arrived.

Richard Brilliant.

Richard pulls the Waiter across and shuts the door. He then goes to take the clothes but the Waiter holds out his hand and gives his gentle cough. Richard goes for his money clip

Waiter I got married in that suit, you know.

Richard gives him five pounds

Richard Yes. Now, Harold, our situation has deteriorated somewhat.
Waiter (*grinning*) Marvellous.
Richard Yes. I need a wheelchair.
Waiter A wheelchair.
Richard For an invalid.
Waiter Has somebody been taken ill?
Richard Several of us but—er—only one requires the wheelchair.

George and Jane enter along the balcony and tap on the window

Richard moves up and opens the window

Waiter Don't they know these suites have doors to them?

George and Jane clamber in

George (*entering*) What's happened?
Jane (*entering*) What did Ronnie want, for God's sake?
Richard Wait a minute. I'm dealing with Harold.
Waiter (*to George*) Are you going to spend *all* your honeymoon to-ing and fro-ing along that balcony?
Richard (*to the Waiter*) Never mind them. Can you fix me up with a *wheelchair*?
Waiter Well, maybe. The hotel keeps a couple for times of emergency.
Richard Time's up, Harold.

Richard pushes the Waiter who stops, coughs and holds out his hand. Richard takes out his money clip

Waiter Ten pounds will suffice.
Richard Oh. You've cleaned me out.
Waiter (*expansively*) That's all right then.
Richard (*surprised*) Thank you, Harold.
Waiter American Express will do nicely.

The Waiter exits

George }
Jane } (*at the same time*) { What's going on? Who's the wheelchair for?
{ Mr Willey, please. What did Ronnie want?
Richard This is worse than Question Time.

The window falls with a bang

God! (*To George*) Now do you want the bad news or the worse news?
George Isn't there any *good* news?
Richard No.
Jane For heaven's sake, give us the bad news.

Richard The bad news is your husband had us followed here by a Private Detective.

Jane and George look aghast

Jane No!
George And you mean there's worse news than that?
Richard Yes. He's the man hanging in our cupboard.
George Oh, my God! (*He looks at the cupboard aghast*)
Jane How could Ronnie behave in such a deceitful way.

George and Richard look at her

Richard How indeed.
George Well, unless it's for me, I don't see where the wheelchair fits in.
Richard George, he's a *Private Detective*! We can't have him discovered in *either* of our suites now, can we? We'll sit him in the wheelchair and put a blanket round his legs.
George Then what?
Richard You push him to Clapham Common, George.
George (*dumbfounded*) Clapham Common?
Richard (*simply*) It's on your way home George. Like I keep saying, the poor man's dead. It won't make any difference to him *where* he's discovered. You can walk there in under the hour. Just dump him in the bushes.
George Dump him in the bushes?!
Jane Look! What about Ronnie?
Richard Yes, that's another good reason for George to emigrate to Clapham Common. I'm afraid I told Mr Worthington a little white lie.
George (*wearily*) What?
Richard That you were about to seduce his wife.
George What?!
Richard He found that hard to believe so he's down at Reception checking if a Mr and Mrs Pigden have booked in.
Jane And we have!
Richard (*delighted*) Suite six-fifty, that's right.
George Mr Willey, do you know what you are?
Richard Well, if I go on like this I could end up the Leader of the Party.

There is a knock at the door. They freeze

(*Sweetly*) Who is it?
Ronnie (*off*) Ronnie Worthington!
George Oh, my God!
Richard (*sweetly*) Coming!

During the ensuing dialogue Richard, George and Jane whisper urgently

Quick!

Richard opens the cupboard door. The Body is still hanging on the inside of the door

Both of you. Get in there.
George Do we have to?
Richard You can either come face to face with the body or face to face with Ronnie.
Ronnie (*off*) Hey!

There is more knocking from Ronnie

George
Jane } (*together*) The body

George pulls Jane across him into the cupboard. Richard picks up the clothes brought in by the Waiter

Richard And while you're in there, put him in Cromwell's wedding suit.
George (*horrified*) Is that really necessary?
Richard Yes. It will delay identification. And hurry up!
George God, you could teach the Mafia a thing or two.

George takes the clothes and Richard shuts the cupboard door. There is more knocking at the door. Richard opens it

Richard (*opening the door*) No need to get impatient.

Ronnie marches in shattered

In the corridor the door of six-fifty opposite has one of its panels kicked in

Ronnie You were bloody right! Mr and Mrs Pigden. Suite six-fifty. (*Disbelievingly*) They're opposite.
Richard (*feigned outrage*) Opposite?! Oh, thats too much.
Ronnie I banged on the door but there was no reply.
Richard Wasn't there?
Ronnie So I kicked the bloody door in!

Richard glances through the open corridor door

Richard Bloody hell!
Ronnie They're not in there though.
Richard Aren't they?
Ronnie Oh, my God!

Ronnie suddenly breaks down. The pent-up emotion is too much for him and he falls to his knees, sobbing. Richard looks totally bewildered as the young man wails and clutches Richard's legs

Richard Get a grip on yourself, Ronnie.
Ronnie It's all my fault!
Richard I'm sure it isn't.
Ronnie Yes, that's why she's gone off with this bloke Pigden. He's better at it than I am.
Richard No!

Ronnie wails more as:

The Manager comes in angrily from the corridor

He is about to knock on the open door when he is confronted by the scene in front of him. Leaving the door wide open, he moves down, aghast

Richard I'm sure you're very good at it. (*He pats Ronnie's head*)

The Manager is appalled

Ronnie No, that's what the trouble is.
Richard What, Ronnie?
Ronnie (*wailing*) I'm no good in bed, Mr Willey!

Richard looks embarrassed. Behind them the Manager looks amazed

Richard I'm sure you're adequate.
Ronnie No. (*Sobbing*) I just can't keep it going.

The Manager is incensed

Richard Don't. You'll only make it harder for yourself.
Manager Mr Willey!!
Richard (*jumping*) Oh, my—! I—er was just explaining—
Manager I'd rather not know what you were explaining.
Richard You can leave him to me. He's got a bit of a problem.
Manager So I heard.

During the above Ronnie has done his best to pull himself together and sits in the chair R

Ronnie I don't usually behave like that in public.
Manager I'm pleased to hear it.
Richard (*to the Manager*) I'll sort it out.
Manager (*angrily*) Well, perhaps you can also sort out Mr Pigden next door.
Ronnie (*rising*) Pigden?
Richard It's all right, Ronnie.
Manager No, it's not all right! The door's been kicked in and the furniture thrown all over the place.
Richard Mr Pigden will pay for any damage.
Manager It's not a question of payment! I can't have this kind of thing going on at the *Westminster Hotel*.
Richard I understand.
Manager I'm all for couples consumating their honeymoon but this is appalling.
Ronnie Honeymoon?!

Ronnie falls to his knees, crying and clasps Richard's legs. Richard sits him in a chair

Richard Try and pull yourself together, Ronnie.
Manager And neither Mr nor Mrs Pigden are anywhere to be seen.
Richard They're probably dining in the restaurant. Why don't you pop down and have a look.

Richard starts to move the Manager away

The Waiter comes through the open door with the wheelchair

Waiter Here we are!

The Manager surveys the Waiter and the wheelchair

Manager What on earth are you doing, Cromwell?

Waiter Answering the call.

Manager (*referring to the wheelchair*) Who is that for?

Waiter Who is it for, Mr Willey?

Richard My young friend there.

Waiter (*to Ronnie*) You're new around here, aren't you?

The Manager is momentarily at a loss

Manager (*to the Waiter*) You can go. (*He assists Ronnie to his feet*)

Waiter Oh. Well—er—

The Waiter looks at Richard. He then points to Richard, points to himself, holds up ten fingers and exits

Manager I don't know who you are young man or what you're doing in Mr Willey's suite at this time of night, but I must ask you to vacate the *Westminster Hotel* as soon as you've got yourself together. (*To Richard*) In future Mr Willey, I think it would be wiser if you were accompanied on these overnight stays by your wife.

The Manager exits into the corridor

Ronnie Bloody hell, I feel lousy.

Richard Go home, you'll feel better.

Ronnie I'm not going home until I've found that bloke, Pigden.

Richard Like I said he's probably downstairs in the restaurant.

Ronnie Right! And when I find him the first thing I'll do is kick him right in the crotch.

Ronnie exits into the corridor

Richard opens the cupboard door

Richard Did you hear any of that?

George Yes, but it was the last bit that brought tears to my eyes.

George steps out holding his groin. Jane follows him

Jane Wasn't Ronnie magnificent?

Richard Magnificent?

Jane The way he declared his love for me. I've never heard him talk like that before.

Richard (*wearily*) Oh, God!

Jane And now he's had the guts to bring his little deficiencies into the open—

Richard Jane, discuss it with your family doctor next week! (*To George*) Did you change his clothes?
George Well, it wasn't easy.

George brings out the Body who is now dressed, very badly, in the Waiter's old wedding suit and wearing the bowler hat. He is still wearing sun-glasses

Richard For heaven's sake!
George It was dark in there.
Richard Stick him in that.

Richard brings the wheelchair forward and George plonks the Body on the seat. Richard surveys him

Well, I suppose we should be grateful it's not November the fifth. (*To Jane*) Right. You go down the fire-escape and get home to Lewisham as fast as you can. (*He opens the window*)
Jane What am I going to say to Ronnie when he gets back?
Richard Tell him Pigden dragged you here by force.
George Thank you!
Jane God, I don't think I can face Ronnie just yet.
Richard Then go back to the House of Commons.
Jane I can't sleep there!
Richard Why not? Everybody else does.

Richard pushes Jane out of the window

Jane exits UR

OK George, this is it. (*He opens the corridor door*) Clapham Common. Walkies with brother Fred. I'll get the lift and hold it for you. Give me thirty seconds. And get our friend a blanket from the bedroom.
George (*opening the bedroom door*) Very well.
Richard And, George, if ever you get married and find yourself in a mess, you can count on me.
George After Ronnie's finished with me I think marriage will be out of the question.

George exits into the bedroom

Richard surveys the room, pats the Body on the cheek and exits

For a moment there is silence and then the Body begins to stir. He shakes his head and then feels his neck which is very painful. He realizes he has sun-glasses on and his hands come up to feel them. He takes the sun-glasses off and looks at them. He then puts them in his top pocket, feels his neck again and moves his head from side to side, which makes him wince. He puts his hands to his neck and rubs it. In doing so he touches the bowler hat. He feels it, takes it off and looks at it puzzled. He replaces the hat on his head and tries to think. He then looks at himself sitting in the wheelchair and tries to work out how he got there. He stands up and then realizes he is wearing strange clothes. He is even more surprised to find his trousers are on back-to-front. He looks around the room

He suddenly remembers the window and points to it as the memory begins to return. He goes to the window and then steps outside. He kneels on the balcony miming what he remembers he did originally. He leans back in through the window and gives a huge smile of satisfaction

Detective Of course! I've got it!

The window suddenly falls on his neck with a loud thump. His eyes close and he slumps

Music

The CURTAIN *falls*

ACT II

The same. Immediately following

After a moment George comes out of the bedroom with a blanket. He throws it over the now empty wheelchair and then moves behind the wheelchair to start pushing. He stops. For a moment his mind is in a whirl. He rushes back to the front of the wheelchair and stares at it. He grabs the blanket and looks at the empty seat. He shakes the blanket to see if the Body will fall out. He then looks beneath the chair and all around it for the Body

Richard hurries in behind George, closing the door

Richard George!
George Ahhh! Don't do that.
Richard I've been waiting by the lift for God's sake. Come on.
George He's gone.
Richard (*impatiently*) Who's gone?
George The Private Detective.

George steps away from the wheelchair and indicates the fact that it is empty. Richard stares for a brief moment

Richard Where is he, George?
George I don't know.
Richard You must have put him somewhere.
George No.
Richard (*grabbing George*) For safety or something!
George No. I went to throw the blanket over him and he wasn't there.
Richard You can't just go and lose a dead body!
George I haven't done anything. He's vanished.

Richard throws his hands in the air and turns away. He sees the Body in the window

During George's ensuing speech Richard moves up and looks at the Body

George You went out to get the lift. I walked into the bedroom, took a blanket off the bed and came back in here. I couldn't have been gone a minute.
Richard (*from the window; flatly*) George.

George looks at Richard who points to the Body between them. George glances down and nods but doesn't take it in

George I was *less* than a minute, Mr Willey. Now he was definitely there when I went into the bedroom. He was sitting there in sun-glasses and Cromwell's wedding suit—

He stops, realizing that he's just seen the Body trapped in the window. He looks at the Body, then he looks at the wheelchair, and then back to Richard

(*Mortified*) Mr Willey!

Richard (*ominously*) George, what have you done?

George I haven't done anything, Mr Willey.

Richard He's back where he was an hour ago.

George I promise you, Mr Willey, the last time I saw him he was sitting in that wheelchair.

Richard Then somebody's on to us.

George On to us?

Richard And, George, I smell blackmail.

George Do you?

Richard Why should anyone stick him back there? Why not call the police or hotel security?

George I knew I should have had this evening at home with Mother.

Richard Don't bring her into it for God's sake. Right. Come on. (*He lifts the window up*).

George What are you doing?

During the ensuing dialogue they get the Body back into the wheelchair

Richard It's back to plan A.

George What's plan A?

Richard Clapham Common.

George But if somebody's on to us!

Richard We've got no other choice, George.

George Yes we have. Plan B.

Richard What's plan B?

George Tell the truth.

Richard Are you mad?

Richard turns the wheelchair and George puts the Body in it

George A lot of people do, you know! It does happen! It's quite simple, too. You and Miss Worthington found a body, that's all.

During the above speech Richard has opened the corridor door

Richard Do you realize what untold suffering would be caused if we resorted to the truth at this stage? Think of poor Mr Worthington. He's in such a state he'd probably chuck himself over the balcony. There's something missing. Sun-glasses.

Richard (*pointing*) They're in his top pocket, Mr Willey. (*He takes them out*)

Richard That'll be another sign from the blackmailer. He's playing games with us, George.

George has replaced the sun-glasses on the "dead" Body

Richard I reckon we'll get a note next.

George A note?

Richard Demanding money.

George Mr Willey, if there is a blackmailer——

The window comes down with a bang. George grabs Richard in terror

—he might follow me to Clapham Common.
Richard That's a chance we'll have to take.
George Oh, will we?!

The Waiter enters through the open corridor door

Waiter Mr Willey!
Richard What do you want?
Waiter (*to Richard*) This is for you. (*He holds out a sheet of paper*)
Richard What is it?
Waiter A note.

Richard goes to take it but immediately stops and looks at George. George clutches Richard's arm. They both look at the Waiter warily

Richard (*to the Waiter*) A note?
Waiter That's right.
Richard Who's it from?
Waiter Me.
Richard (*surprised*) You.
Waiter That's right.

Richard and George exchange another look. Richard takes the note and reads it

Richard (*reading*) "For supplying one wheelchair, ten pounds." (*He angrily crumples up the note*)
Waiter (*seeing the Body*) Your brother's taken a turn for the worse, has he, Mr Pigden?
George Yes. Poor Fred's passed on—(*quickly*) passed out.
Waiter It was all that dancing that did it.
Richard Very likely.
Waiter (*to Richard*) As a matter of interest why has he changed into my wedding suit?
Richard Fred's going to a wedding.
Waiter (*surprised*) Is he? (*To George*) He's already been to yours today.

George nods dumbly

Richard He's going to his other brother's now.
Waiter (*delighted; to George*) Have you got *another* brother?

George nods dumbly

Richard Yes. Bert.
Waiter (*to Richard*) And Bert's getting married on the same day as him?
Richard Yes! Bert and George are twins.
George Oh, my God!

George sits inadvertently on the Body. He leaps up with a yell and we see that he has sat on the Body's upturned hand which has "goosed" him. George rubs his backside, gives the Body a remonstrative glance and slaps the Body's hand

Waiter I say! (*He taps his watch*) It's a bit late for Bert to be having a wedding ceremony, isn't it?

Richard It's performed in conjunction with Midnight Mass.

Richard starts to propel the Waiter out as:

Ronnie storms in through the door

George quickly pushes the wheelchair and Body into the corner by the bedroom door

Ronnie Mr Willey! I can't find Pigden or my wife anywhere.

Waiter (*to Ronnie*) Good-evening, sir.

Ronnie Who the hell are you?

Richard The richest man in the hotel.

Richard pushes the Waiter out into the corridor

Ronnie They're hiding somewhere.

Richard Why not go home, sleep on it, and sort it out in the morning.

Ronnie strides into the room

Ronnie I'm going to sort it out *now*! Starting with George bloody Pigden!

Ronnie stops on seeing George with his back to him standing in the corner. There is a fractional pause

George, hiding his face from Ronnie, pushes the wheelchair in front of him and through the door

Richard smiles encouragingly at Ronnie

Richard (*to Ronnie*) That was Doctor Livingstone.

Ronnie assimilates this

Ronnie And who was the guy in the wheelchair?

Richard Oh, just somebody's brother.

Ronnie Whose?

Richard (*after a slight pause*) Mine. Harrington Willey. Doctor Livingstone is with him permanently. Poor Harrington. The brain's completely gone.

Ronnie You kind of forget other people's problems when you're up to your eyes in your own.

Richard puts his arms around Ronnie's shoulders

Richard You go home. Mrs Worthington's been faithful to you, I just know she has.

The Manager comes in behind them. He stops, amazed

And when you get home, Ronnie, go up to your wife and say—I believe in Willey.

The Manager is staggered

Manager Mr Willey!

Richard just closes his eyes

Richard I'm busy!

Manager Mr Willey I would like to remind you, most forcibly, that when you booked into this hotel, you intended to depart immediately for the House of Commons.

Richard Something popped up.

Manager No doubt! However, I'm sure it's now been dealt with so nothing further need detain you—or Ronnie.

Ronnie (*angry again*) Don't you take that attitude with me!

Richard I think the Manager's got a point, Ronnie.

Ronnie He shouldn't allow his hotel to be used for adultery in the first place!

Manager Adultery?

Richard Now, Ronnie—

Ronnie Mr and Mrs bloody Pigden opposite.

Manager Yes, well Mr Pigden's got a lot to answer for.

Ronnie He bloody well has.

Manager I've just told him I want a full explanation for the damage done in six-fifty.

Richard I'm sure you'll get it. Come on, Ronnie.

Ronnie (*to the Manager*) Have you just been talking to Pigden?

Manager By the lift.

Ronnie Bloody swine.

Ronnie rushes out into the corridor

Richard Ronnie! (*To the Manager; angrily*) Now look what you've done!

Manager And I've also told Mr Pigden I want him and his wife out of this hotel immediately.

Richard Mrs Pigden's gone and Pigden's on his way. You've ruined their honeymoon, you know that!

Manager And another thing. Why is Mr Pigden pushing his brother around the hotel in a wheelchair?

Richard To get some fresh air. For Fred not George. Fred came over very unwell. Far too much champagne. So George is pushing him home.

Manager (*surprised*) To Felixstowe?

Richard No, Lewisham!

George rushes in, looking petrified

George Mr Willey!

Richard Pigden! You're supposed to be on your way to Clapham Common! (*To the Manager*) Via Lewisham.

George He's risen!

Richard (*assimilating*) Risen. Who's risen?

George The fellow in the wheelchair.

Richard What the hell are you talking about?

George The fellow in the wheelchair!

Manager Your brother, Fred?

Richard (*to the Manager*) Would you leave us alone, please?

George He stood up!

Richard tries to assimilate this

Richard Who did?
George The fellow in the wheelchair!
Richard What?!
Manager Well, Fred was only inebriated, surely.
Richard (*to the Manager*) Thank you!
George I was just about to push him into the lift and he *stood up.*
Richard He *can't* have done!
Manager Why on earth not?!
Richard (*to the Manager*) Please! (*To George*) What did you do?
George I ran like hell.

Richard looks furious

Richard And what did Fred do?
George (*almost crying*) He went down with the lift.

Richard looks even more furious

Manager Really! He'll probably be sick all over Reception.

The Manager angrily rushes out into the corridor slamming the door closed

George He's come back to haunt us, Mr Willey.
Richard Oh, shut up. He's not dead, that's what it means.
George (*relieved*) God, do you think so?
Richard And that's not good news.
George Oh, it must be good news, Mr Willey, surely.
Richard For our erstwhile dead body, yes. But not for us.
George It's wonderful news for us. I don't have to push him to Clapham Common! And I can go home and relieve Nurse Foster.
Richard George! Don't you realize if he's alive he'll be able to verify everything about Miss Worthington and me. (*Suddenly remembering*) Hey, did you see Mr Worthington in the corridor just now?
George Yes, he looked very cross!
Richard Well, you're all right there. He's looking for Mr Pigden.
George I know!
Richard And he thinks you're Doctor Livingstone.

George goes to speak but immediately stops

George Doctor Livingstone?
Richard Look, I must get to that detective before he bumps into Ronnie and spills the beans—(*Suddenly*) God!
George What?
Richard I've told Ronnie that that Detective is my crazy brother, Harrington.
George Makes a change. You've told everybody else he's my drunken brother, Fred.

Richard Now, if Jack Baker turns up before I get back——
George Who's Jack Baker?
Richard Our Private Detective! You just keep him here.
George Oh, my goodness.
Richard And if Ronnie returns before I do—
George Yes?
Richard God help you!

Richard opens the door to leave but:

The Waiter comes in pushing the wheelchair

Waiter I've got a complaint.
Richard It's probably your age.

Richard hurries out, leaving the door open

Waiter (*to George*) I went to a lot of trouble to get this wheelchair for your brother, Fred.
George Thank you very much!
Waiter And instead of him using it I find it going up and down in the hotel lift.
George Fred doesn't need it any more.
Waiter I'll take it back then. (*He starts to go*)
George Thank you.

The Waiter stops

Waiter But I'll keep it on stand-by for the next emergency.

The Waiter exits

George Thank you! (*He closes the door*)

Oh, my goodness.

There is a knock on the door

(*Angrily*) What is it now?

George opens the door. Pamela Willey is standing in the doorway. She is wearing a hat and a jacket over a summer dress and carrying an overnight case and a handbag

Pamela (*surprised*) Hello, George!

Pamela enters

George is looking at her open-mouthed. She kisses him on the cheek and walks in front of him surveying the room. George, in a trance, closes the door

(*Turning to George*) Well, this is a pleasant surprise.
George (*dumbly*) Mrs Willey.

Pamela puts her case down and then smiles at George

Pamela What are you doing here?

George (*dumbly*) Mrs Willey.
Pamela Yes, George?
George (*dumbly*) Mrs Willey.
Pamela Shouldn't you be at the House of Commons with Richard?

George goes to answer but stands there with his mouth open

(*She looks at her watch*) Or at home with your mother.
George I came over—

Pamela waits for him to continue but he doesn't

Pamela Came over what, George?
George Here.
Pamela Yes.
George To help Mr Willey. He left something here. Some papers. He sent me. He—House of Commons. Me here.
Pamela Yes. I expect Richard's up to his eyes in it, is he?

George hesitates and then is only able to emit a foolish laugh

You've had a long day, have you, George?

George nods

There's nothing wrong, is there?
George (*expansively nonchalant*) No.

There is a knock at the door

(*Yelling*) Ahhh!

George leaps forward as he yells and Pamela steps back, startled. George smiles at her and indicates that nothing untoward has happened

(*He calls*) Who is it?
Waiter (*off*) Room Service.

George opens the door

George (*as he opens the door; to Pamela*) Room Service.

The Waiter enters with the wheelchair

Waiter I thought you might need this after all.
George No! No, I'm fine now, thank you. It's just left me with a bit of a limp.

George limps around for Pamela's benefit

Yes, that's much easier. (*To the Waiter*) Thanks for your trouble.

Still limping, he gives the Waiter a five pound note. While burbling on he thrusts several more on to the surprised Waiter. Pamela steps in fascinated

You've been really helpful. I couldn't have managed without you. It's so much better. I feel fitter than I have for years. Thank you.

By now George has put the Waiter into the wheelchair and shoves him out through the open door. There is the sound of a loud crash from down the corridor

Waiter (*off*) Ahhhh!

George closes the door and looks innocent

George Now where were we, Mrs Willey?
Pamela Have you had a fall or something, George?
George Er, yes. (*He limps around*) I fell off one of the back benches.

Pamela looks surprised

(*Quickly changing the subject*) Mrs Willey, I thought you were in the country.

Pamela takes off her hat and puts it on the chair

Pamela I was but I decided to drive up and give Richard a little surprise.
George I think it'll be a big one, actually.
Pamela Lovely.

Pamela picks up her overnight case. George picks up her hat and offers it to her as he speaks

George (*brightly*) So you just want to see Mr Willey, say a quick "hello" and then drive back to the country, yes?
Pamela (*laughing*) Don't be silly, George. I'm staying the night.
George The night?!
Pamela Yes.
George No! I mean, Mr Willey's got an all-sight nitting—an all-night sitting.
Pamela I know. I decided I wanted to hear him speak tonight. How's the Government getting on by the way?
George What government?
Pamela In the debate?
George Oh, *that* Government. Fine. Fine. Limping nicely.
Pamela (*moving to the bedroom door*) Well, I can either go over to the Commons and watch Richard from the Visitors' Gallery——

Pamela goes into the bedroom

George (*mortified*) No, you can't do that!

Pamela returns minus her case

Pamela —or sit here with some sandwiches and a glass of wine and watch the debate on TV.
George No, you can't do that either!
Pamela Why on earth not?
George Because—it's much quieter next door.
Pamela (*surprised*) Next door?
George The suite next door. It's mine.

Pamela Yours?
George Yes. Mine. Next door.

George rushes into the bedroom

Pamela Are you staying at the hotel as well?

George rushes back with her case

George It's a treat from Mr Willey. Come on! (*He thrusts the hat on her head*)
Pamela What do you mean, "come on".
George Next door. Come on. The two of us! (*He pushes her but she stops*)
Pamela What are you talking about?
George (*hysteria creeping in*) The two of us. We might never get another chance like this!

Pamela is totally befuddled as she surveys George who is in a state of frenzy

Pamela Chance for what, for heaven's sake?
George To make mad passionate love!
Pamela (*amazed*) Mad, passionate——
George Love, Mrs Willey!

He drops the case, grabs her and kisses her wildly. While Pamela struggles George runs his hand up and down her leg to indicate wild passion. He finally releases her

Pamela (*incredulously*) George!
George You've driven me wild for years, Mrs Willey. (*He kisses her again and repeats the leg-stroking*)
Pamela I can't believe this is happening.
George I know exactly how you feel.

He kisses her again. She stands there breathless

Pamela George—!
George God, you're lovely. (*He kisses her again*) Don't fight it, Mrs Willey.
Pamela Who's fighting it, George?!

She grabs him, kisses him and strokes his leg. Finally she releases the struggling George

Is this why you've been behaving so strangely, George?
George You've noticed, have you?
Pamela And all these years you've been——
George Holding it in, yes.
Pamela Come on!

She grabs his hand and takes him to the hall door

George No! Safer to use the window.
Pamela The window?
George We don't want to bump into anyone, do we? (*He opens the window*)
Pamela (*clambering out*) Good thinking, George.

George Quickly!

Pamela stops and leans back in

Pamela Oh, George. My nightie and things.
George (*forcefully*) You don't need a nightie with me!

George starts to clamber out of the window but she stops him

Pamela Of course I do.
George All right but we're wasting valuable time. (*He gets Pamela's case and handbag*) Quickly, Mrs Willey. (*He joins her on the balcony*)
Pamela George, do you think this is utter madness?!
George I bloody well do!

They exit along the balcony UL

There is silence for a moment

Richard hurries in from the hall closing the door behind him

Richard I can't find that damned detective any——! (*He looks around*) George!

Suddenly the window bangs shut. Richard goes to window and opens it. He looks off UL

(*He calls*) George!

Jane appears on the balcony from UR

Jane (*tapping Richard's shoulder*) Mr Willey!
Richard (*yelling*) Ah!

Richard straightens up and bangs his head

Ahh!

Jane clambers in

Jane I'm sorry, Mr Willey.
Richard What on earth are you doing back here?
Jane I got lost.
Richard What?
Jane Well, I went down the fire-escape like you said—
Richard (*impatiently*) Yes?
Jane And I got out at the wrong floor.
Richard God!
Jane Well, I was trying to find my way downstairs—
Richard Yes?!
Jane And Ronnie saw me.
Richard Ronnie?!
Jane It's all right. I've managed to give him the slip. What have you done with that dead detective?
Richard When last seen he was taking the lift down to Reception.
Jane What?

Richard Our dead detective isn't dead.
Jane Not dead?
Richard Although if he meets up with Ronnie some of us might be. You get back to the House of Commons—(*he takes her to the window*)—and don't get lost this time. I'm trying to get to that detective before Ronnie does.
Jane What's Mr Pigden doing?
Richard God knows but he'd better not be lying down on the job, that's all.

Jane exits along the balcony UR

Richard hurries to the hall door and opens it

The Detective is standing there holding his neck, and about to knock. He is still wearing the bowler hat

Richard Oh!
Detective Oh!
Richard May I—er—be of any assistance?
Detective To tell you the truth, I'm not sure. The thing is—well it all sounds a bit silly really—but I seem to have lost my memory.

Richard takes this in

Richard (*broadly*) My dear fellow, *do* come in. (*He ushers the Detective into the room. Sympathetically*) Lost your memory? How very distressing.
Detective Yes, I can't even remember my name.
Richard (*thrilled*) That's terrible.
Detective Yes. Or what I'm doing in this hotel.
Richard That's awful!
Detective Yes. And I've got a splitting headache.

The window bangs shut. They both react. Richard smiles at him. The Detective feels his neck as a vague memory stirs

Richard (*hastily*) Well, you mustn't go wandering about the place in that condition, sir. Certainly not.

He sits the Detective on the divan

You might bump into anybody. (*Quickly*) Anything. Put your feet up and lie back.

Richard lies him back at an angle and starts to move to the corridor door

Detective (*sitting up*) You're very kind.

Richard returns and lies him back

Richard Always ready to give a helping hand.
Detective It really is a most peculiar feeling. It's just that suite six-four-eight seemed ... (*He suddenly sits up alert*) We don't know each other, do we?

Whenever the Detective gets his "flashes" of memory he is always alert and dangerous

Richard Never set eyes on you, sir. But when my colleague returns he'll be able to assist you. He's a doctor.

Richard lies him down and starts to move to the door. The Detective sits up

Detective A doctor, that's lucky.

Richard returns and lies him back

Richard Yes, isn't it.

George enters through the window from UL

(*Hurrying to George*) Ah, here's the very man.
George Oh, thank God you're here, Mr Willey.
Richard I was wondering where you'd got to, Doctor.
George (*pressing on*) The most devastating thing has happened——
Richard (*interrupting*) First things first, Doctor Livingstone.
George She's waiting next door for me and she thinks I'm going to make mad—(*confused*) Doctor Livingstone?
Richard You may be able to help this poor fellow.

Richard indicates the prone Detective. George turns to look

George (*yelling*) Ahh!

The Detective sits up and turns to George

(*Relieved*) Oh, I thought he'd snuffed it again.

The window bangs shut. George clutches Richard

Richard (*to the Detective*) You'll be in very good hands with Doctor Livingstone. He's a neurologist.
George Oh, my God! (*He almost collapses*)
Richard It's all right, Doctor. This poor fellow's lost his memory.

George looks blank for a moment then he turns to the Detective

George (*brightly*) Have you?
Detective It's crazy. I can't even remember who I am.
George (*thrilled*) That's terrible.
Richard Yes. He can't recall what he's doing in this hotel either.
George (*thrilled*) That's awful.
Richard Yes.

The Detective stands up, once more alert

Detective I seem to remember something about this room, though!
Richard }
George } (*together*) Oh.
Detective (*pointing to the window*) And that window!
Richard }
George } (*together*) Oh.
Richard (*to George*) I think you should put the patient to bed, Doctor.
George That's a good idea.

Richard In the suite next door.
George That's not such a good idea.
Richard (*surprised*) But this suite is likely to get crowded, Doctor.
George It's getting pretty crowded next door.
Richard (*annoyed*) I don't quite follow you, Doctor.
George Well, that's what I was trying to tell you—I—er—I—(*Lifting the Detective*) I'll explain after I've put my patient to bed—in here.
Richard All right!

As Richard moves to the bedroom:

Ronnie comes furiously through the hall door

George quickly leans on the Detective's bowler hat, pushing it down over his eyes and sitting him on the divan again

Ronnie My wife's given me the slip and I still can't find Pigden.
Richard (*to Ronnie*) Why not try suite six-fifty again. Mr Pigden might have moved back in.
Ronnie Six-fifty, yes!
George (*rising*) No!

George stops Ronnie. Richard is confused again

Richard Surely, it's worth Ronnie trying next door, Doctor Livingstone.
George No, it isn't! Mr Pigden's not there.
Richard (*annoyed again*) He might be! It's better for Ronnie to keep trying!!
George NO! I was with Mr Pigden only five minutes ago.
Richard (*very surprised*) Were you?
George Yes!
Ronnie Where?
George In the hotel indoor swimming pool.
Richard Swimming pool?!
Ronnie Swimming pool?!
George We were doing a few lengths together.
Ronnie I'll give him a few lengths. (*He moves to the door*)

The Detective rises, his memory stirred by the sight of Ronnie

Detective (*to Ronnie*) Hang on a second. Have you ever seen me before?
Ronnie Yeah, you're Mr Willey's crazy brother, Harrington!

Ronnie exits into the corridor

George and Richard look mortified at each other. George pulls Richard across him to explain to the Detective

Detective (*blankly*) Your crazy brother, Harrington?
Richard Well, you see, it's like this——
Detective (*moved and amazed*) I'm your brother!
Richard Yes, you are.
George Oh, my God! (*He sits in a chair* DR)
Richard It's all right, Doctor, Harrington's just a bit confused.

George *Harrington's* confused.

Richard Yes. As to why we didn't explain to Harrington our relationship in the first place.

Detective Yes.

Richard Yes. You see—you've been ill for some time. The memory keeps coming and going. (*To George*) You've got a name for it, haven't you, Doctor?

George (*with feeling*) Oh, yes, I've got a name for it, all right.

There is a knock on the hall door

George Oh, God!

Richard See who that is, will you, Doctor.

George Could I just discuss something personal with you very quickly, Mr Willey?

Richard Later, Doctor. You open the door while I put Harrington to bed.

Detective You're very kind.

Richard That's what big brothers are for, Harrington.

Detective Are you sure it's not "Jack"?

Richard (*flatly*) Jack?

Detective It's a name that keeps coming into my head. "Jack"!

Richard That's because you work in a garage, Harrington.

Richard takes the Detective into the bedroom

There is a further knocking from the door

George (*apprehensively*) Who is it?

Maid (*off*) It-is-the-maid.

George opens the door

The Maid enters

Make-bed-now.

George No, the bed's occupied. And the bed in six-fifty's occupied too.

Maid Non capisco.

George That makes two of us.

George pushes the Maid out

Pamela appears on the balcony from UL *and taps on the window*

Oh, no! Sssh!

George indicates for her to go back, but Pamela taps louder at the window. George lifts the window. Pamela is now wearing a negligèe. She starts to come in and George tries to stop her

George (*whispering urgently*) I told you to stay next door.

Pamela What's taking you so long? You only came back to borrow Richard's dressing gown.

George I couldn't find it.

Pamela Well, come on! I've ordered champagne and oysters. (*She pulls him to the window*)

George But, Mrs Willey ... !
Pamela Do as your told, George!

She grabs him and kisses him as:

The Waiter pops his head through the window. He is carrying a tray on which is champagne and oysters

Waiter Champagne and oysters!
George (*yelling*) Ahhh!

Pamela and George break hurriedly from their embrace

Pamela They're for suite six-fifty.
Waiter I know, but that's empty so I reckoned you'd all be in here.

George looks up to heaven

George Take it next door!
Waiter Right! I'll go the way I came, shall I?
George Yes!
Waiter Right! (*To Pamela*) Are you on the bride's side or the groom's? (*He indicates George*)

George almost dies

Pamela I beg your pardon?
George Just do as your told!
Waiter Right!

The Waiter exits along the balcony UL *with the tray*

Pamela Come on! (*She climbs out of the window*)
George Mrs Willey, I'm a bit worried about Mr Willey.
Pamela George, it's an all-night sitting. He'll be in the Commons till breakfast time.
George (*looking at the bedroom*) But he might pop in—I mean he might pop over—

As George moves towards the corridor door, the window comes down with a bang on Pamela's head. George stands transfixed for a moment with his back to the window. He can't bring himself to look. He then slowly turns and sees the prostrate Pamela

Oh, my God!

George hurries over to the window and lifts it. He pulls Pamela into the room

(*Whispering urgently*) Mrs Willey! Mrs Willey!
Pamela (*holding her head*) Ohh!
George (*realizing she's all right*) Oh, thank goodness!
Pamela (*smiling faintly*) What a kiss, George! (*She slumps into George's arms*)
George Mrs Willey!

There is a knock on the hall door. George staggers around with Pamela who keeps slipping through his arms. There is more knocking from the hall door. George opens the cupboard door and bundles Pamela in. There is more knocking from the hall door

All right, all right! (*He opens the door*)

Nurse Foster (Gladys) is standing there. She is wearing a private nurse's uniform and carrying her coat and a handbag. She strides past George into the room and looks around

George is dumbstruck. He closes the door and gapes at her

Gladys So what have you got to say for yourself, Mr Pigden?
George (*dumbly*) Nurse Foster.
Gladys Your poor mother's worried to death, you know that!
George (*dumbly*) Nurse Foster.
Gladys I'm surprised at you, really I am. You've always been so reliable until today.
George Nurse Foster.
Gladys And what do you mean by getting married without telling anybody?

George goes to speak but stops

Your mother's in a right state, I can tell you. I told her I wouldn't leave this hotel until I got some sense out of you.
George Tell Mother I'll explain when I get home.
Gladys Nurse Foster wants an explanation *now*, Mr Pigden.

The cupboard door opens. Pamela steps out and comes face to face with Gladys. Pamela is still only semi-conscious

Pamela (*as she steps out*) What a kiss, George. (*To Gladys*) Sorry, wrong room.

Pamela returns to the cupboard, closing the door. Gladys looks at George who can only emit a silly giggle

Gladys Was that your new wife?
George No, that's Mr Willey's old one. (*He pulls her down from the cupboard*)
Gladys (*amazed*) Mr—you mean that woman's your Minister's wife?
George Yes.
Gladys She said "What a kiss, George".
George It was something like that, wasn't it?
Gladys How many women have you got here?
George I've lost count!
Gladys Mr Pigden!
George Please go home, Miss Foster! Mr Willey's likely to come in any minute and so's everybody else.

Gladys sits purposefully in the chair R

Gladys And where's this bride of yours then?

George (*lifting her*) She's not my bride. She's one of the secretaries over there.

Gladys One of the —?!

George Shhh!

Gladys What have you been doing, Mr Pigden?!

George (*hissing*) I've been doing my best for everybody, Miss Foster! Now go home to Mother!

Gladys Not without you!

George Right! Then come next door. (*He lifts her up and pulls her across him*)

Gladys Next door?

George Suite six-fifty. It's mine. Come on.

Gladys What on earth for?

George To make mad passionate love.

Gladys Mad passionate——?

George Love, Nurse Foster!

George grabs her and kisses her wildly. As Gladys struggles George rubs his hand sexily up and down her leg. Finally George releases her

Gladys (*amazed*) Mr Pigden!

George God you're lovely!

George grabs her and kisses her passionately once more. He then releases her

Gladys Have you gone mad?

George Yes, you've driven me there!

George grabs Gladys and kisses her. He then releases her

Don't fight it, Nurse Foster!

Gladys Who's fighting it, Mr Pigden?!

She throws her handbag over her shoulder, grabs him and kisses him wildly, running her hand up and down his leg. Finally she releases him. George is almost destroyed

I always knew there was more to you.

George Yes, there's not much left of it now though.

Gladys What about Mrs Willey and that secretary?

George Who wants them now you've turned up?

Gladys Come on! (*She grabs him and pulls him to the door*)

George No! We always use the window.

Gladys The window?

George (*pulling Gladys to the window*) It's safer. Tell you what—you go first. I'll take all my clothes off then I'll come along the balcony and join you.

Gladys George!

George I want to be all naked and alluring. (*He waggles his bottom seductively*)

Gladys All right. You'll find me in the same condition.

She waggles her bottom and clambers out as George collects her handbag

George Quickly, Nurse Foster.
Gladys (*leaning back in*) I think you can call me "Gladys".
George Why? Oh, "Gladys". Yes, lovely. (*Suddenly*) Gladys, don't lean in like that!
Gladys (*leaning back*) Why not?

The window descends with a bang

Gladys laughs, blows George a kiss and exits UL *along the balcony*

George (*to himself*) George, you've been wasting yourself all these years.

He hurries to the cupboard and opens it. Pamela is beginning to come to

Mrs Willey!
Pamela Are you coming in to join me, George?
George No, you've got to go home.

The bedroom door opens and Richard steps out with his back to George, talking to the unseen Detective

Richard You just lie there and relax, Harrington.

At the sound of Richard's voice, George steps into the cupboard with Pamela and closes the door

(*Looking around*) George? George!

There is a knock at the hall door

(*Sweetly*) Who is it?
Waiter (*off*) Room Service.

Richard opens the door

The Waiter enters DL

Richard What do you want?
Waiter Sign, please (*He produces his pad*)
Richard What's this for?
Waiter Champagne and three dozen oysters. Suite six-fifty.
Richard I didn't order that.
Waiter No. Mr Pigden did.
Richard Mr Pigden ordered it?
Waiter That's right.

During the ensuing dialogue the cupboard door falls open behind Richard's back. Pamela is leaning up against the back wall, semi-conscious with a happy smile on her face. George is standing spread-eagled facing her with his back to the room. Pamela has her arms around George's waist and her head on his shoulder. George looks around, horrified and sees Richard and the Waiter, who don't see him. George steps out of the cupboard and gingerly starts to close the door

Richard He can't have done. Go away.
Waiter He did, I tell you.

Richard You've made a mistake.
Waiter No, I haven't. Suite six-fifty.
Richard Suite six-fifty?

Richard turns to see George just about closing the cupboard door

Richard George!
George (*jumping*) Ahh!

George bangs the cupboard door, turns, puts his hands up and moves away from the cupboard

Richard What the hell are you doing?
George Coming out of the cupboard.
Richard What the blazes were you doing in there?
George Seemed like a good idea at the time.
Richard Silly fool. And did you order champagne and oysters for suite six-fifty?
George (*laughing foolishly*) Yes.
Richard Why?
George Seemed like a good idea at the——
Richard (*interrupting*) Oh, shut up! Now, Harold, I'd—
Waiter (*ignoring Richard. To George*) Here, it's taking you a long time to get cracking on your honeymoon, isn't it?
George Yes!
Waiter And was that other one the mother-in-law?
George Yes! (*He pushes the Waiter to the door*)
Richard (*to Waiter*) Before you go, Harold I'd like to ask a little favour—
Waiter (*rubbing his hands*) Lovely!
Richard Do you by some chance have any sleeping pills?
George Sleeping pills?
Richard (*to George*) For your brother, Fred. He's starting to remember too much. (*To the Waiter*) The stronger, the better.
Waiter I'm sure one of the chambermaids will have some.
Richard Get them here as soon as you can.
Waiter No sooner said than done.

The Waiter coughs and holds out his hand. Richard feels for his money clip but remembers it's all gone

Richard George, do the honours, will you?

George brings out a money clip

George (*to the Waiter. Holding out a five pound note*) You needn't think you're going through my salary as well.
Waiter The night is young.

The Waiter takes the money and goes

Richard I'll finish putting Harrington to bed while you stand guard here in case Ronnie returns.

George (*stopping Richard*) Mr Willey! I've got to tell you something! (*He looks at the cupboard and then back to Richard*)
Richard (*impatiently*) What?
George (*hardly able to say it*) Mrs Willey.
Richard (*not hearing*) What?
George Mrs Willey.
Richard Mrs Willey?
George Ssh!
Richard What about Mrs Willey?
George She's in the cupboard!

Richard's mind races as he tries to assimilate George's remark but his face remains impassive

Richard (*flatly*) Pamela's in the cupboard.
George Yes. In her nightie.
Richard Pamela's in the cupboard in her nightie.
George Yes.
Richard Drinking a cup of cocoa, I suppose.
George No!
Richard (*flatly*) What's she doing in the cupboard in her nightie?
George She's waiting for me to take all my clothes off.

There is a pause then Richard suddenly bursts into uncontrolled laughter. Finally he pats George affectionately on both cheeks while George just stands there looking blank. Richard staggers to the divan, laughing. The phone rings. Richard lifts the receiver

Richard (*on the phone. Still laughing*) Hello? . . . (*He stops laughing*) What do you want now, Nurse Foster?!
George Oh, my God! (*To Richard*) Let me talk to her.

Richard indicates for George to be quiet

Richard (*on the phone*) Look, tell Mr Pigden's mother he'll be home before midnight. . . . Well, where *are* you then? (*He listens for a moment. To George; flatly*) What's Miss Foster doing in suite six-fifty?

George hesitates

George She's waiting for me to take all my clothes off.
Richard (*after a pause*) Then what?
George She's expecting me to make mad passionate love.
Richard (*on the phone*) Nurse Foster, I hope this service of yours is provided on the National Health! (*He slams the phone down*) I suppose the champagne and caviare were for Nurse Foster?
Richard No. They were for Mrs Willey.

Richard hesitates then looks at the cupboard and back to George

I tried to tell you, Mr Willey.

Richard opens the cupboard and Pamela steps out

Pamela Oh, Richard, I've had such a bang.

Richard remains calm, turns Pamela around, gently pushes her into the cupboard and closes the door

George (*hurrying to Richard*) She had a bang on her *head*, Mr Willey.

Richard I don't need to know the position, Pigden!

George She was hit by the window.

Richard Was that before, during or after?

George Mrs Willey wanted to give you a little surprise, that's all.

Richard She's done that all right!

George So please get her dressed and make her go home before she meets that Detective or Ronnie.

The Waiter enters with a bottle of sleeping tablets

Waiter Sleeping pills!

Richard I'll deal with you later, Pigden.

Richard goes to take the bottle of pills but the Waiter removes the bottle and holds out his hand

Pigden!

George hands over a five pound note which Richard gives to the Waiter. Richard takes the pills and hands them to George

(*To the Waiter*) And you can go now. We won't be requiring your services any more tonight.

Waiter You never know your luck.

Jane rushes through the open hall door

Jane Mr Willey!

Richard (*to the Waiter*) Don't go away.

George Miss Worthington! Your husband's still on the rampage.

Jane And so's the Prime Minister, I'm afraid.

Richard Oh my God!

Waiter I don't think there's room for the Prime Minister in here.

Richard and George glare at the Waiter

George What's *happened* Miss Worthington?

Jane Well, when I got over there the debate was getting out of hand and the House was in an uproar.

Richard But what *happened*?

Jane Well, the P.M. was starting to get a bit flustered. Then one of the Labour Back Benchers stood up and said "It's a pity the Prime Minister's lapdog isn't in the House to protect him".

Richard Lapdog?

George That's you, Mr Willey.

Richard glares at George

Jane Well, of course, when the Prime Minister realized you weren't there, Mr Willey, steam started coming out of his head. I think he actually kicked your Chief Whip's ankle.

George Oh, Mr Willey!
Waiter Things are starting to hot up now, aren't they?
Richard Be quiet!
Jane Look, I've got to get back. If the Labour bench knew I was warning
you, Mr Willey, I'd be out on my ear.
Richard You're a dear sweet girl. We'll both go.

Richard moves to go but George grabs him

George No! You go Miss Worthington. Mr Willey will be there in two
minutes. But first he's got to handle something—*here!*

*George flicks his finger surreptitiously across Richard's "crotch" to indicate
the cupboard. Richard and Jane look down at George's wild gesticulation*

The Detective enters from the bedroom and points dramatically at Richard

Detective Hey!

They all look at him

I've remembered why I came to the *Westminster Hotel*——

*Richard, George and Jane exchange a quick worried glance and look back at
the Detective*

—it's no good, it's gone again.
Richard Go and lie down.

Richard pushes the Detective into the bedroom

Jane What's that Private Detective doing in your bedroom?
Richard Don't worry. George is dealing with him.
Waiter (*to George*) Is your brother Fred a Private Detective?

George glares at the Waiter

George (*pleading to the Waiter*) Go away!
Richard (*to George*) Go and give your brother those pills, George. We've
got to get back to the Commons!

Richard takes Jane's arm. George grabs Richard

George But first you've got to *handle* something.

He repeats his "flicking". Richard slaps his hand

Richard I'll make a brief speech, chuck a few insults at the Labour Front
Bench and be back in ten minutes.
George (*grabbing Richard*) The world could come to an end in ten minutes!

The Detective returns and points a finger at Jane

Detective I know you, young lady, don't I?

Richard and Jane exchange a brief glance

Jane (*brightly*) I don't think so.

Detective Your face is very familiar.
George She's a very familiar young lady.
Waiter How do you know? You haven't had a chance to find out. (*He chuckles*)

George glares at the Waiter

Detective (*to Jane*) I know I've seen you somewhere.
Richard Of course you've seen her. She's married to Doctor Livingstone.
Waiter (*looking around*) Doctor Livingstone?

George clips him around the head. He smiles and pretends to the others to be smoothing down the Waiter's hair

Detective (*to Richard*) And you're sure my name's not "Jack"?
Richard Positive.
Detective "Willey" doesn't seem to fit either.
Waiter Bloody hell!

Richard, George and Jane glare at the Waiter

Richard (*to the Waiter*) Buzz off.
Detective And, you know, Richard, it's damn strange but I just don't feel as though I'm your brother.
Waiter He's *Mr Willey's* brother?

George clips him around the head. He smiles at the others and tidies the Waiter's hair

Richard You take Harrington into the bedroom, Doctor.
Waiter Harrington? I thought his name was—

The Waiter stops in mid-sentence and, before George can do anything, he hits his own head. They turn to look. The Waiter smiles at them and tidies his own hair

Richard Doctor, will you put Harrington to bed and give him his sleeping pills! (*To Jane*) Come on!
George (*grabbing Richard*) Mr Willey, I'm more worried about who's going to handle—!

George repeats his "flick" gestures. Richard slaps George's hand

Richard (*interrupting*) We're *all* worried, Doctor. Just stay with the patient until he drops off.
Detective Richard, I have no strong feelings about the doctor either.
George (*grimly. To Richard*) Well, I've got strong feelings about a lot of people.

George pushes the Detective into the bedroom

Richard (*pointedly*) Then clean out the cupboard here and the bed in six-fifty! I'll be back as soon as I can.

Richard moves to go but the Waiter stops him

Waiter Here, Mr Willey! How can his (*he points to George*) brother be your (*he points to Richard*) brother as well?

Richard We all had the same mother but George and Fred and Bert had a different father from me.

The Waiter looks at George. George leans his head against the wall and sobs. The Waiter moves to George and taps him on the shoulder

Waiter Just a minute, what's your relation with Mr Willey then?

George (*pointedly. At Richard*) Very strained!

Richard (*to George*) Go and look after Fred, George!

George All right! But I'm very glad that Fred, Bert and I had a different father from you!

George exits into the bedroom

Jane Come on, Mr Willey. The P.M. will be going potty.

Richard Right. (*To the Waiter*) You can cope till I get back, can't you, Harold?

Waiter Oh, yes, I reckon there's a lot of mileage in this yet.

Jane Hurry up, Mr Willey.

She opens the door to leave but slams it shut again

Ronnie!

Richard Ronnie!

Jane Looking funny!

Richard (*to Jane*) Window!

Richard pushes past the Waiter banging the Waiter's head on the cupboard door

Richard rushes to the window and exits along the balcony UR

Waiter Is Ronnie one of the good guys or the bad guys?

Jane He's the worst!

Jane pushes past the Waiter, banging the Waiter's head on the cupboard door

There is a knock on the hall door

Waiter Coming. (*He goes to open the door*)

Jane (*moving back to the Waiter*) Don't open that door!

It's too late

Ronnie steps into the room, dressed in only a towel and his shoes. His hair is soaking wet

Jane can't make the window, so she opens the cupboard door (the semi-conscious Pamela is happily clutching the clothes rail) and goes in

As the cupboard door closes Ronnie comes into the room, glowering. The Waiter surveys him, blandly

Waiter Good-evening, sir. Are you looking for the hotel swimming pool?

Ronnie I fell into the hotel swimming pool.

The Waiter nods

Waiter I trust you're staying here. It's for hotel guests only.
Ronnie (*ominously*) Where's Mr Willey?
Waiter Ah, he's just this second left.
Ronnie I didn't see him.
Waiter No, he took the usual route, through the window.
Ronnie (*getting hysterical*) Well, I'm looking for his Secretary, George Pigden!
Waiter Ah, yes, Mr Pigden. He was here a moment ago, too.
Ronnie In this room?
Waiter Yes.
Ronnie Did he have a young woman with him?
Waiter He did indeed. His new bride.
Ronnie New bride?!

Ronnie bursts into tears, falls to his knees and clasps the Waiter around the waist. The Waiter stands there at a total loss. He doesn't know whether to comfort Ronnie or not. Finally, the Waiter, to be on the safe side, puts his hands on his head

Waiter Yes. Funny thing, the Pigdens and Mr Willey all seem to have disappeared at the mention of the name "Ronnie".
Ronnie Right! (*He moves to the window*)
Waiter If I bump into any of them, sir, shall I say who called?
Ronnie Yes, Ronnie! (*He clambers out of the open window*)
Waiter Right. Ronnie. (*Realizing*) Ronnie?!
Ronnie (*leaning back in*) What is it?
Waiter Just hang on a second.

There is a pause of about two seconds and then the window descends with a bang on Ronnie's neck

Ronnie Ohhh!
Waiter Oh dear, oh dear, oh dear!

The Waiter pulls the curtain across the window and then knocks on the cupboard door

Waiter (*calling*) The bad guy's bitten the dust.

Jane comes out of the cupboard. Pamela is seen clutching the clothes rail

Jane (*closing the cupboard door. To the Waiter*) Thanks. (*She runs to the hall door and then stops*) Oh, I don't know if anybody knows but there's a lady hanging in the cupboard.
Waiter A lady?
Jane In a négligé.
Waiter Oh, *that* lady. She's your mother, isn't she?

Jane goes to speak but decides there's no time and exits

The Waiter takes out his pad and pencil

(*Writing. To himself*) For eliminating one bad guy, ten pounds.

The Waiter exits into the corridor, closing the door

The curtains are opened by a dazed Ronnie

Ronnie Oh, my bloody head! (*He extricates himself from the window*) Bloody swine, Pigden!

He starts to move to the corridor door but stops on seeing the telephone directories beneath the table

Of course, Pigden's home address!

Ronnie starts to sift through the appropriate book for "Pigden" as:

George tip-toes out of the bedroom door

George gently closes the door, hurries to the cupboard and opens the door, not having seen Ronnie

Ronnie (*finding the number*) George Pigden!
George (*yelling*) Ahhh! (*He slams the cupboard door closed*)
Ronnie (*reading*) Twenty-five, Kenilworth Avenue, Wimbledon.

George turns, closing the cupboard door. Ronnie throws the telephone directory down and moves towards the hall door

George (*worried*) What are you doing, Ronnie?
Ronnie Going round to Pigden's house.
George No, I'm not home! I mean *he's* not home. He's in the swimming pool, remember.
Ronnie The only one who's been in the swimming pool is me! He's done a bunk, the crafty devil.

He opens the door to go but George grabs him and pulls him across him into the room

George No!
Ronnie Let go of me, Doctor Livingstone!
Geogre Please!

George drops to his knees and grabs Ronnie's towel

Ronnie I'm going round to Pigden's house!

The Manager enters furiously

He looks for George and stops dead on seeing George on his knees pulling at Ronnie's towel

George No! No, please! Please, please, please!
Ronnie Let go!
George No, Ronnie, you can't leave me!

The Manager reacts

Ronnie, please! Don't go.
Ronnie I'm going to give him what he's been asking for!

The Manager reacts

George No! I want you to stay with me, Ronnie!
Manager Stop that!
George Ahhh!

George falls on his face, releasing Ronnie who secures his towel. George remains on his knees

Manager If you don't leave this hotel I shall call in our Security Officer and have you removed in handcuffs!
George Quite right.
Manager (*to Ronnie*) And if Ronnie doesn't vacate the hotel immediately—
Ronnie I'm vacating it all right.

Ronnie strides past George but George, still on his knees, grabs Ronnie's towel from behind

George No, please!

George is pulling the towel and Ronnie is trying to hold it up

Please, Ronnie, Ronnie!
Manager Now, stop that! (*He smacks George's hand*) That's naughty! Stop it, I say!

The Manager gets between them to separate them but George, thinking it's Ronnie, pulls at the Manager's trousers which come down to his ankles

Ahhh!

The Detective enters from the bedroom. He now has the pyjama jacket on as well as the trousers, but still wears the bowler hat. He is very alert

Detective I've got it!
George Ahhh!

The mêlée disperses with George falling to his knees, the Manager pulling his trousers up and Ronnie re-securing his towel

Manager (*pointing at the Detective. To George*) You said he'd gone!
Detective Baker! That's my name. Baker!
George Go back to bed!
Manager He's not staying here! (*To "deaf Fred", shouting*) You have another wedding to go to.

The Detective reacts

Detective I've been married to Mrs Baker for fifteen years.
Manager I'm getting Security!

The Manager exits into the hall struggling with his trousers

George (*to Ronnie*) You mustn't mind poor old Harrington.

Ronnie I don't give a damn about Harrington.
Detective No, *Jack Baker.*
Ronnie (*realizing*) Jack Baker?
Detective That's me.
Ronnie Wait a minute! (*He takes off the Detective's bowler hat. Astonished; to George*) This bloke's my Private Detective. What the hell's happened to him?
George (*lightly*) Nothing untoward as far as I know.
Detective (*pointing*) You're Ronnie Worthington!
Ronnie I bloody well know who I am.
Detective Mrs Worthington!

George looks worried

Ronnie Do you know where my wife is?
Detective Oh, yes. (*He goes to speak then yawns and slumps to the floor*)
George My patient should really be in bed.
Ronnie (*stepping across the Detective*) You keep quiet, Doctor Livingstone.
George Of course.
Detective I can see right up your towel, Mr Worthington.

Ronnie furiously kneels down again and grabs the Detective

Ronnie (*to the Detective*) Where's my wife?
Detective (*suddenly bright*) Window!

Ronnie stops shaking the Detective and looks at the window

Ronnie My wife went out the window?

The Detective moves up to the window

Detective Window yes.
Ronnie Right. (*He starts to move to the window*)
Detective Hey, I remember everything now!

Ronnie stops and turns. George is looking desperate. The Detective opens his mouth to speak but yawns and curls up once more on the floor to the R of the chair with his head resting on it. Ronnie opens the window and steps outside

Ronnie (*to George*) Right, first I'm going to find my wife and then I'm going to drag her round to Pigden's house.
George There's no need to do that, Ronnie!

Ronnie leans in through the open window

Ronnie I'll have it out with both of them.
George In that case, Ronnie, just hang on a second!

There is a pause during which the window does not fall

Ronnie What the hell is it?
George Er—

George hesitates and looks up, then stamps on the floor, hoping the window will fall. It doesn't. Ronnie is still waiting for George to speak. George hesitates, stamps again and then exhibits a few Karate blows. Ronnie watches bemused. Still the window doesn't fall

Ronnie (*finally*) Oh, bloody hell!

Ronnie exits UR *of the balcony*

George turns away furious that the window didn't fall—the window falls with a bang. George looks angrily back at it

> *Gladys, wrapped in a towel, appears outside from the balcony* UL

She taps on the window. She is carrying Pamela's clothes. George opens the window but prevents Gladys from coming in

George Nurse Foster, I told you to stay in suite six-fifty.
Gladys (*angrily*) I found these clothes in a neat pile at the foot of the bed.
George (*taking the clothes*) They're Mrs Willey's, thank you. (*Realizing*) Where are *your* clothes?
Gladys In a neat pile at the foot of the bed! I trust Mrs Willey's leaving.
George Definitely.
Gladys And what about that secretary?
George She's already left. You wait for me next door.
Gladys (*seeing the Detective*) Who's that?
George Him? Oh, he comes with the suite. You get back, Gladys. I'll sort out Mrs Willey.

He turns to go towards the cupboard as the window comes down with a bang on Gladys neck. For a moment George is transfixed and can't bring himself to look. Finally he does

> Oh, my God!

There is a knock on the hall door

> Ahhh!

George, in his fright, throws Pamela's clothes in the air

Detective (*sitting up*) I think I've got it!
George Shut up!

George smacks the Detective across the back of the head and he subsides. There is a further knocking at the door. George quickly lifts the window and pulls Gladys in. She is very dazed

Gladys Oh, my goodness me.
George Oh, thank heavens!
Gladys What happened, George?
George The usual.
Gladys Oh, what a kiss! (*She falls into George's arms*)

There is more knocking at the hall door

George (*sweetly*) Who is it?
Richard (*off*) It's me for God's sake. Open the door, George.

George, trying to support Gladys, opens the door

The debate is going disastrously—(*He stops on seeing Gladys in George's arms*) Who the hell's that?
George Nurse Foster.
Richard You don't hang about, do you? (*He sees the Detective*) Why isn't he in bed?!
George (*angrily*) I'm not sure!
Richard How many pills did you give him?
George One.
Richard One pill?
George No, one bottle.
Richard Look, I can't stay, the debate is going disastrously for the Government over there.
George Things are going disastrously for everybody over here.

The window falls with a bang

Richard ⎫
George ⎭ (*together*) Ahh!

In his fright, George drops Gladys

Richard Have you seen my wife home?
George No she's still in the cupboard. (*He collects up Pamela's clothes*)
Richard What?!
George And you've got to get her dressed. And Ronnie fell into the swimming pool and the Manager's gone to get the Security Officer.

Richard grabs Pamela's clothes from George and then opens the cupboard door pulling Pamela out. He is acting very much the severe husband

Out you come, Pamela!
George In you go, Gladys.

George pushes Gladys, who has not been noticed by Pamela, into the cupboard

Pamela (*to Richard*) Good-evening, Richard.
Richard (*firmly*) Put your clothes on, Pamela, and then go home.

He thrusts Pamela's clothes at her and pushes her towards the bedroom but she stops on seeing the Detective

Pamela Who's that?
Richard That's George's brother, Fred.
George Oh, no! (*He collapses on to the divan*)
Pamela I didn't even know George had a brother.
Richard Fred called in to see George before he goes to Felixstowe to see Bert.
Pamela Bert?
Richard That's George's other brother. Now go and put your clothes on!
Pamela (*to George*) You've got *two* brothers?
George (*glaring at Richard*) I've got three actually but I'm not talking to the third one.

Pamela What's happened to—er—Fred?
Richard He had too much to drink at George's wedding.
George (*holding his head*) Oh, my God! (*He buries his head in his hands*)
Pamela George's *what*?!
Richard Yes, George got married this morning, didn't you, George?
George (*growling*) I suppose I did, yes!
Pamela (*moving to George*) Well, you sly old thing, George.

George emits a nervous giggle

So what's your bride's name?
George (*tersely*) Felixstowe!
Pamela What?!
Richard He met her in Felixstowe. Her name's Ivy. Now, hurry up!!
Pamela Well, Ivy doesn't seem to be very much in evidence. (*To George*)
Where exactly *is* the lucky lady?
George (*unhelpfully*) I don't know.
Pamela What?

Richard is getting desperate

Richard He doesn't know *exactly* where she is. They've been larking around
playing hide and seek.
Pamela Hide and seek?
Richard Just get dressed, Pamela, and go home!

The window opens and Ronnie comes in still dressed in a towel and shoes

Richard hastily pulls Pamela behind him

Ronnie She's given me the bloody slip again.
Richard Mr Worthington, do you mind!
Ronnie Yes, I *do* bloody mind.
Pamela Richard!
Richard Yes, my sweet?
Pamela Who is this?
Ronnie Never mind who I am. (*To the Detective*) You'd better pull yourself
together. (*To George*) Can't you give him something, Doctor?

*Pamela who is standing next to George, looks amazed at him. George hesitates
and then decides to look around for the "doctor"*

Oi (*trying to get George's attention*) Doctor Livingstone!

*Pamela looks amazed at George again. George looks around for "Doctor
Livingstone". He then gets up and searches under the divan for the "doctor"*

The window bangs shut

Richard }
George } (*together*) Ahhh!
Ronnie (*to George. Referring to the Detective*) You'd better wake him up. I
need him for my evidence.
Pamela Evidence?

Ronnie Now where's my wife hiding?

Ronnie exits into the bedroom

Richard (*to Pamela*) Ronnie and his wife are playing hide and seek too.
Pamela Who exactly is Ronnie?
Richard Ronnie's on the bride's side of the family. He's married to one of Ivy's cousins.
George Oh, my God! (*He walks to the divan and collapses*)
Richard Sweet boy, Ronnie.
Pamela He called George "Doctor Livingstone".
Richard That's right.
Pamela Why did he do that?
Richard (*to George*) Why did he do that, George?
George (*slowly standing up*) Because that's who I am! Doctor Livingstone! Fred and Bert's brother and half brother to Trickey-Dicky!

George thrusts his face at Richard giving him a stoney glare

Ronnie enters distraught, slamming the door

Ronnie God knows where my wife is!
Pamela (*laughing*) It's not all that serious, is it?
Ronnie Not serious?!
Pamela It's only a game.
Ronnie Only a game, Mr Willey!

Ronnie bursts into tears, falls to his knees and grabs Richard

Richard There, there, you give in and have a good cry.
George (*crying*) I think that's what we'd all like to do. (*He sits on the divan*)
Pamela Get Ronnie a drink, George.
Ronnie (*becoming alert*) George?
Pamela Yes. (*She points to George*) Let Mr Pigden here get you a drink.

Ronnie looks slowly at George. George emits a nervous giggle. Ronnie moves to George with pent-up fury

Ronnie (*ominously*) Are you George Pigden?

There is a pause

George I beg your pardon?
Ronnie Are you bloody George Pigden?
George Ah, bloody George, yes.
Ronnie (*to Richard*) He's been screwing my Jane.

George buries his head in his hands

Pamela What?!
Richard I think it's a phrase used in carpentry.
Ronnie It's a phrase used in the *Westminster Hotel*! He's the one (*he points at George*) who's been trying to get to bed with my wife.
George I assure you I've been trying no such thing with anybody's wife.

Pamela No, I suppose even George would stop at having an affair with his wife's cousin.

Ronnie Look, it's no good—(*He stops*) Wife's cousin?

Pamela Your wife is one of Ivy's cousins, isn't she?

Ronnie Ivy?

Richard Of course! You're Ronnie *Worthington*! That explains everything.

Ronnie Does it?

Richard Yes! Tell him, George.

Everybody looks at George. For a moment George looks blank

George (*finally*) Well, you see, Ronnie—your wife has a mother, doesn't she?

Ronnie Yes.

George (*with finality*) Good!

George realizes that he is expected to continue

Well your wife's mother has a sister who has some children and one of them is a daughter called Ivy who got married today to me.

There is a pause

Ronnie I don't get it.

Richard It's all very simple, Ronnie! George invited your wife here to join in the wedding reception.

Ronnie (*to George*) So why wasn't *I* invited?

George It was just close family, Ronnie.

Ronnie I think I'd better sort it out with Jane.

Pamela Who's Jane?

George No trick questions, please.

Richard Jane is Ronnie's wife, isn't she, Ronnie?

Ronnie Yes. (*To himself as he goes*) I'm married to the sister of a brother whose wife has a sister whose mother has a daughter called Ivy who's married to the man who works for Mr Willey.

As Ronnie exits his towel catches on the door handle and slips to the floor

For a moment we see his naked rear view as he turns into the corridor. Everybody is agog. George removes the towel from the door handle and looks down the corridor. Ronnie has gone

George (*to Richard*) I hope Ronnie looks down before he gets home to Lewisham.

Richard Now please get dressed, Pamela! I've got to get back to the Commons.

As Richard moves to the corridor door:

Jane hurries in

Jane (*to Richard. Overjoyed*) I thought you'd like to know that Ronnie and I are going to be OK!

Richard Good!

Jane We just met in the corridor and I could tell that he was really pleased to see me.

Jane exits happily, closing the door

Richard That was Jane. (*Desperately*) Pamela! Put your dress on and then make your own way to the Visitors' Gallery.

Pamela No, I think I'd rather like to stay here and meet Ivy.

Richard and George stare blankly at her for a moment then look blankly at each other and then back to Pamela

Richard
George (*together*) Meet Ivy?

Pamela To congratulate her.

Richard Darling, Ivy's very busy playing hide and seek.

Pamela I only want to *meet* the girl.

Richard (*blustering*) But she doesn't want to meet you! (*Feigning sudden anger*) And I don't want *you* to meet *her*.

Pamela Why on earth not?

Richard Because I really didn't take to Ivy at all! (*Furiously*) I'm sorry, George, but I have to say that I found her belligerent, bombastic and totally without charm!

George stands there considering this

George (*finally*) Well *I* like her.

Pamela (*amazed*) Richard! That wasn't a very nice thing to say.

Richard Well, that's how Ivy struck me. She's bloody ugly, George!

Pamela Richard!

Richard I'm a forthright man, Pamela.

Pamela Did you let Ivy know how you feel about her?

Richard Most definitely, didn't I, George?

George Yes, he said to her, "You're bloody ugly, Ivy".

Pamela Well no wonder the poor girl's hiding. Go and find her, George. (*She moves to the bedroom*)

Richard Pamela!

Pamela You go ahead, Richard. The Prime Minister will be getting impatient.

Pamela exits into the bedroom

Richard George, I think our situation has deteriorated somewhat.

George Deteriorated?! You don't know what you've done to me! And what about poor Nurse Foster?!

Richard She'll keep, she's in the cupboard.

George I've got to get her home! And God knows what we'll tell Mother.

Richard Never mind Nurse Foster and your mother. Mrs Willey won't leave this suite until we produce Ivy.

George In that case Mrs Willey is in for a hell of a long wait!

Richard Wait a minute! We *can* produce Ivy.

George How for heaven's sake?

Richard Nurse Foster! In the cupboard!

George takes a moment for the implication to sink in

George Oh, no!
Richard If Nurse Foster's prepared to make mad passionate love to you she'll do anything.
George Mr Willey!
Detective (*sitting up*) Mr Willey!
George Shut up!

George whacks him across the back of the head and the Detective subsides. Richard pushes George to the cupboard

Richard You tell Nurse Foster what she's got to do.
George Don't you think you've ruined enough lives for one evening?
Richard George, the Prime Minister's waiting for me!

There is urgent knocking on the hall door

George He's come to collect you!
Richard Get in there!

He pushes George into the cupboard. Gladys is seen hanging on to the rail. Richard closes the door

Richard (*sweetly*) Who is it?
Waiter (*off*) It's your favourite waiter.

Richard opens the door

  The Waiter hurries in

Waiter I got here as fast as I could.
Richard Nobody sent for you.
Waiter No, but I knew there was bound to be some crisis or other. You need a Mrs Ivy Pigden, don't you?
Richard How did you know that?
Waiter I was listening at the keyhole. (*He calls off*) Come on! (*To Richard*) Close your eyes!

  The Maid enters

She wears a bright but ill-fitting dress and a hat with a veil. The Waiter pulls her into the room and thrusts her at Richard

Richard (*referring to the Maid*) Who's that?
Waiter This is your erstwhile chambermaid, Maria.
Richard What are you talking about?
Waiter Mrs Willey won't leave until she's met Ivy. (*Pleased*) Well, meet Mrs Ivy Pigden.

The Maid smiles coyly. Richard looks aghast towards the cupboard

Richard (*horrified*) Get her out of here, quickly!

Richard grabs the Maid as:

Pamela comes in from the bedroom now dressed

Richard pulls the Maid behind him

Pamela (*as she enters*) Now, George, have you found—Oh! You still here, Richard?

Richard tries to mask the Maid

Richard I thought I'd hang on for you, my precious.

Richard puts his arms around Pamela and turns her away. At the same time he indicates for the Waiter to remove the Maid

Pamela I told you I'll be over when I've said "hello" to George's bride.
Waiter (*to Richard*) You see.

The Waiter pushes the Maid forward into the centre of the room

Pamela (*seeing the "Bride"*) Oh.
Richard (*glaring at the Waiter*) Say "hello", Ivy!

Pamela is rather surprised at the sight of Ivy. Pamela looks at Richard

Richard (*quietly*) I told you she was bloody ugly.
Pamela Richard! (*To Ivy*) Hello, Ivy.
Richard Well, there you are, you've said "hello to Ivy"

George comes out of the cupboard with Gladys and marches down to beside the Maid

George I'd like you to say "hello" to Ivy.

Everybody reacts suitably. Richard nearly dies

Richard (*flatly*) Pamela has already said "hello" to Ivy.

Richard indicates the Maid. George looks at her. The Maid puts her arm through George's arm and smiles at him. George nods

Gladys What's going on, George?!
George (*indicating Richard*) Ask the vicar!
Pamela (*referring to Gladys*) Who exactly is that, George?
Gladys I'm Nurse Foster!
Pamela Nurse Foster?
Richard They couldn't afford a Matron of Honour so they got the next best thing. Anyway, you've met Ivy.
Pamela Yes. (*To the Maid*) You must be so thrilled, Ivy.

The Maid doesn't say anything and then looks to the Waiter for guidance. Everybody then looks at the Waiter

Waiter Ivy doesn't speak any English!

George and Richard both close their eyes. George collapses on to the divan and Richard onto the chair

Pamela No English?
Richard (*tersely*) Didn't you mention that to Pamela, George?
George (*tersely*) I forgot.
Richard (*rising*) Ivy's Spanish.
Waiter Ivy's Italian.
Richard Half Spanish, half Italian.
Pamela (*to George*) You met her in Felixstowe, George?
Gladys (*to George*) Felixstowe?
George (*rising*) Yes, Felixstowe! On the beach.
Richard She'd swum over from Venice!
Gladys Venice?
George (*to the Maid*) Waiter take you back to suite six-fifty, Ivy!
Richard Yes, off we all go then!

They all prepare to move as:

  The Manager comes in from the corridor

Manager I'm sorry to interupt whatever's going on in her but—if this room
  is not vacated within five minutes I have a Security Guard in the corridor
  who will arrest all of you. And *when* you leave, Mr Pigden, take your
  brother with you.
George Yes, of course. We're both going to Bert's wedding.
Gladys |
Pamela | (*together*) Bert's wedding?
Richard The Pigden's are potty about weddings.
Manager The Pigdens are potty, full stop! (*To the Waiter. Angry and
  exasperated*) And why do I keep finding you here Cromwell?
Waiter Just lucky, I suppose.
Manager (*amazed. To the Maid*) And what are you doing in here dressed
  like that, Maria?!
Maid Bed. (*She curtsies to the Manager*)
Pamela Maria? (*To George*) I thought her name was Ivy.
George It is. Ivy Maria.

They all look at George who smiles politely

  *The Manager, exasperated, grabs the Maid and exits with her into the
  corridor*

Pamela Richard?
Richard Yes, my sweet?
Pamela Why did the Manager take Ivy off like that?
Richard It's an old Italian custom.
Waiter Mr Willey.
Richard Yes, Harold?
Waiter Shall I continue to receive my emolument from Mr Pigden?
Richard Yes, Harold.

George goes to get some money from his pocket

Waiter (*to George*) I think a monthly Banker's Order is the best thing.

The Waiter exits

Gladys I don't know what I'm going to tell your mother about all this, Mr Pigden.
George For a start you can tell her I've met the woman I'm going to marry.
Gladys (*frostily*) Have you, Mr Pigden?
George I have, Nurse Foster.
Gladys And who's that, may I ask?
George You!

Gladys looks at him dumbfounded

Gladys Me?!
George You've been magnificent this evening. (*He takes her hands in his*)
Gladys (*overcome*) Have I, Mr Pigden?
George What a woman!
Gladys I think you're pretty magnificent yourself, George.
George Do you really, Gladys?
Richard Give her a kiss for God's sake!

He pushes George into Gladys's arms. George takes her arm and as they exit, Gladys's towel slips to the floor and for a brief moment we see her naked rear view

Obliviously, George and Gladys exit, looking into each other's eyes

Richard That reminds me!
Pamela What?
Richard I've got to face the Prime Minister.

Music as:

Richard hurriedly pulls Pamela across him and they exit into the corridor

CURTAIN

FURNITURE AND PROPERTY LIST

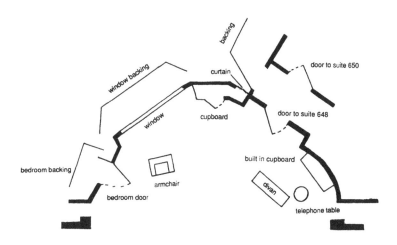

ACT I

On stage: Divan. *On it:* Richard's briefcase containing papers
    Armchair
    Built-in cupboard. *In it:* radio, television
    Table. *On it:* telephone, London directories
    Tables (optional)
    Ornaments (optional)
    Pictures (optional)

Off stage: Trolley with champagne, caviare and oysters on it **(Waiter)**
    Briefcase **(George)**
    Dress **(Waiter)**
    Pile of clothes **(Waiter)**
    Wheelchair **(Waiter)**

Personal: **Richard:** watch, money clip with six five pound notes and a fifty pence
    piece. Sun glasses in pocket
    Jane: watch
    Waiter: watch, pad, sheet of notepaper, key
    Manager: watch, pass key

ACT II

On stage: As Act I

Off stage: Blanket **(George)**
Wheelchair **(Waiter)**
Overnight case, handbag **(Pamela)**
Tray containing champagne and oysters **(Waiter)**
Bundle of clothes **(George)**
Handbag **(Gladys)**
Sleeping tablets **(Waiter)**

Personal: **Waiter:** pad, sheet of notepaper
Pamela: watch, bracelet
Gladys: watch
George: wallet containing five pound notes

LIGHTING PLOT

Practical fittings required: four wall lamps
Interior: The same scene throughout

ACT I

To open: General interior lighting, practicals on

No cues

ACT II

To open: General interior lighting, practicals on

No cues

EFFECTS PLOT

Please see note on page vi concerning the use of copyright music.

ACT I

Cue 1   **Richard** switches the radio on   (Page 3)
Voice as script followed by snatches of music including military music

Cue 2   **Richard** switches off the radio   (Page 4)
Cut music

Cue 3   **Jane** presses a button on the radio   (Page 5)
Intro music of "Love And Marriage"

Cue 4   **Richard:** ". . . suitable song than that."   (Page 5)
Snatches of music

Cue 5   **Jane:** "I think I feel sick   (Page 5)
Radio plays soft music

Cue 6   **Jane** turns off the radio   (Page 6)
Cut music

Cue 7   **Richard:** "Good!"   (Page 8)
Telephone rings

Cue 8   The **Waiter** hesitates and starts to go   (Page 22)
Telephone rings

Cue 9   **Richard:** ". . . get him into six-fifty."   (Page 24)
Telephone rings

Cue 10   **George:** ". . . that's all that's left."   (Page 27)
Telephone rings

Cue 11   The **Detective**'s eyes close and he slumps   (Page 38)
Music

ACT II

Cue 12   **George** shoves the *Waiter* out through the open door   (Page 46)
Sound of loud crash from the corridor

Cue 13   **Richard** staggers to the divan, laughing   (Page 59)
Telephone rings

Cue 14   **Richard:** "I've got to face the Prime Minister."   (Page 77)
Music

MADE AND PRINTED IN GREAT BRITAIN BY
LATIMER TREND & COMPANY LTD PLYMOUTH

Lightning Source UK Ltd.
Milton Keynes UK
UKOW06f0131071215

264243UK00001B/20/P